THE ULTIMATE DOG TRAINING BIBLE

Everything You Need to Raise a Happy, Well-Behaved Dog — from Puppy to Senior, with Positive Reinforcement and Practical Tips for Every Stage

Susan White

© Copyright 2024 - All rights reserved.

The content contained within this book may not be reproduced, duplicated, or transmitted without direct written permission from the author or the publisher.

Under no circumstances will any blame or legal responsibility be held against the publisher, or author, for any damages, reparation, or monetary loss due to the information contained within this book. Either directly or indirectly.

Legal Notice:

This book is copyright protected. This book is only for personal use. You cannot amend, distribute, sell, use, quote, or paraphrase any part, or the content within this book, without the consent of the author or publisher.

Disclaimer Notice:

By reading this document, the reader agrees that under no circumstances is the author responsible for any losses, direct or indirect, which are incurred as a result of the use of the information contained within this document, including, but not limited to, — errors, omissions, or inaccuracies.

TABLE OF CONTENTS

Preface 1

Introduction 4
   The Importance of Training 4
   How Dogs Learn: The Basics of Positive Reinforcement 7
   Setting Realistic Training Goals 9

Chapter 1: Preparing Your Home for a New Dog 13
   Puppy-Proofing Essentials 13
   Creating a Welcoming Environment 15
   Gathering the Right Supplies 17
   Planning Feeding, Sleeping, and Play Areas 19
   Preparing the Family 21

Chapter 2: Understanding Your Dog's Development 24
   Puppy Developmental Stages 24
   Teenage Years and Training Challenges 26
   Training Older Dogs: Starting Fresh 28
   Understanding Dog Body Language 30
   Building a Bond and Trust 32

Chapter 3: Crate Training and Safe Spaces 34
   Benefits of Crate Training 34
   Choosing the Right Crate for Your Dog 36
   Starting Crate Training: Step-by-Step 37
   Crate Training for Alone Time and Independence 39
   Troubleshooting Common Issues 41

Chapter 4: Potty Training Essentials 43
Establishing a Routine 43
Using Positive Reinforcement for Potty Training 45
Recognizing Signals Your Dog Needs to Go 46
Handling Accidents with Patience 48
Troubleshooting Potty Training Problems 50

Chapter 5: The Power of Positive Reinforcement 53
Basics of Positive Reinforcement 53
Common Mistakes to Avoid 55
Timing and Consistency in Training 57
Keeping Training Sessions Engaging 58
Balancing Treats and Praise 60

Chapter 6: Basic Obedience Commands 62
Teaching Short Commands (Sit, Stay, Come) 62
Essential Commands for Everyday Life 63
Reinforcing Commands through Repetition 65
Transitioning Commands to Real-Life Scenarios 67
Correcting Command Confusion 69

Chapter 7: Socializing Your Dog 71
Importance of Early Socialization 71
Socializing with People, Dogs, and New Environments 73
Managing Socialization for Older Dogs 74
Introducing New Pets or Babies to Your Dog 76
Avoiding Overstimulation 78

Chapter 8: Problematic Behavior and Solutions 80
Instinctual vs. Learned Behavior 80
Addressing Jumping, Barking, and Begging 82
Solutions for Chewing, Digging, and Biting 83
Setting Boundaries and Routines 85

Correcting Behavior with Positive Techniques 87

Chapter 9: Advanced Obedience and Fun Commands 89

Advanced Commands: Heel, Stay, Leave It 89
Building Focus and Impulse Control 91
Teaching Tricks: Roll Over, Spin, High Five 92
Exercise and Enrichment Activities 94
Tailoring Commands for Challenging Environments 96

Chapter 10: Health, Hygiene, and First Aid 98

Basics of Dog Grooming and Hygiene 98
Dental Health and Nail Care 100
Handling Common Health Emergencies 101
Recognizing When to See the Vet 103
Basic Dog First Aid Kit 105

Chapter 11: Outdoor Adventures and Safety 107

Hiking and Camping with Your Dog 107
Water Safety: Swimming and Boating 108
Preparing for Long Walks and Runs 110
Safety Tips for Different Seasons 111
Avoiding Common Outdoor Hazards 113

Chapter 12: Diet and Nutrition for Every Stage 115

Choosing the Right Food for Your Dog's Age 115
Feeding Schedules and Portion Control 117
Special Diets and Food Sensitivities 118
Tips for Feeding Senior Dogs 120
Treats, Snacks, and Healthy Rewards 122

Conclusion 124

PREFACE

Dear Reader,

Congratulations on taking the first step towards a rewarding journey of understanding, training, and bonding with your dog. Whether you're a new puppy parent, a rescue dog adopter, a dog lover seeking to improve your relationship, a busy professional looking for efficient training techniques, or a pet caregiver and community dog enthusiast, this book is designed to be your comprehensive guide through every stage of your dog's life.

"The Ultimate Dog Training Bible: Everything You Need to Raise a Happy, Well-Behaved Dog — from Puppy to Senior, with Positive Reinforcement and Practical Tips for Every Stage" is more than just a book. It's a testament to the incredible bond that can be formed between humans and dogs when we take the time to understand their needs, behaviors, and unique personalities.

This book is founded on the principle of positive reinforcement, a method that emphasizes rewarding good behavior rather than punishing the bad. It's a method that not only works but also builds a relationship based on trust and mutual respect. It encourages your dog to think, to make choices, and to take joy in learning.

In the following chapters, you'll find practical advice on everything from preparing your home for a new dog, understanding your dog's development, crate training, potty training, socializing your dog, addressing problematic behavior, to health, hygiene, and first aid. Each chapter is designed to provide you with the knowledge and tools you need to raise a happy, well-behaved dog.

But this book is not just about training your dog; it's also about training yourself. It's about learning patience, consistency, and the art of understanding canine body language. It's about realizing that each dog is unique and that what works for one might not work for another. It's about celebrating small victories and not getting disheartened by setbacks.

Training a dog is not a linear process. It's a journey filled with ups and downs, successes and failures, laughter and perhaps a few tears. But through it all, you'll find that the bond you share with your dog strengthens, and the love and respect you have for each other deepens.

As you embark on this journey, remember to be patient with your dog and yourself. Change takes time, and learning is a process. Celebrate the small victories, learn from the setbacks, and always move forward with love and respect.

This book is your guide, your mentor, and your companion on this journey. It's here to provide you with knowledge, to answer your questions, to offer solutions, and to reassure you that you're not alone. It's here to remind you that you're capable of raising a happy, well-behaved dog.

So, dear reader, let's embark on this journey together. Let's learn, grow, and create lasting, positive changes in our dogs' lives. Let's build a relationship with our dogs that's based on trust, respect, and mutual understanding. Let's raise happy, well-behaved dogs.

Here's to our journey together,

Susan White

INTRODUCTION

The Importance of Training

The journey of dog ownership is a rewarding one, filled with moments of joy, laughter, and the kind of companionship that only a four-legged friend can offer. But like any worthwhile journey, it comes with its fair share of challenges. One of the most significant of these challenges is training your dog.

Training your dog is about so much more than teaching them to sit, stay, or fetch. It's about communication, understanding, and building a relationship that's based on mutual trust and respect. It's about creating a bond with your dog that's so strong, it transcends the barriers of species and language. Training is an essential part of responsible pet ownership and is crucial for your dog's overall well-being.

The importance of training can't be overstated. It's not just about having a well-behaved dog; it's about providing your dog with the guidance and structure they need to feel secure and confident. Dogs, like humans, thrive on routine and consistency. They need to know what's expected of them and what they can expect from us. Training provides this consistency and helps to establish a routine that your dog can rely on.

Training also helps to prevent behavioral problems. Many common behavioral issues, such as excessive barking, chewing, or digging, can be prevented or mitigated through proper training. By teaching your dog appropriate behaviors and providing them with mental stimulation, you can help to curb these unwanted behaviors.

Moreover, training is a form of mental stimulation for your dog. Dogs are intelligent creatures, and they need mental exercise just as much as they need physical exercise. Training exercises your dog's mind, keeps them mentally sharp, and helps to prevent boredom and associated destructive behaviors.

Training also enhances safety. A well-trained dog is less likely to run off and get lost or get into dangerous situations. Basic commands like "come," "stay," and "leave it" can potentially save your dog's life in certain situations.

Perhaps one of the most significant benefits of training is that it strengthens the bond between you and your dog. Training is a form of communication, and the more effectively you can communicate with your dog, the stronger your bond will be. Training sessions give you and your dog the opportunity to spend quality time together and understand each other better.

Now, when we talk about training, we're talking about positive reinforcement training. This method of training is based on the principle that dogs will repeat behaviors that are rewarded. It's a humane and effective way to train your dog that builds trust rather than fear.

Positive reinforcement training involves rewarding your dog for performing a desired behavior. The reward can be anything your dog finds enjoyable - a treat, a toy, praise, or even a belly rub. The key is to reward your dog immediately after they perform the desired behavior, so they make the connection between the behavior and the reward.

This method of training is not only effective, but it's also enjoyable for both you and your dog. It's a win-win situation. Your dog gets a reward they love, and you get a well-behaved dog. Plus, it's a great way to build a positive relationship with your dog.

As you embark on your training journey, it's important to set realistic training goals. Remember, training is a process, and it takes time. Don't expect your dog to learn everything overnight. Be patient, be consistent, and celebrate small victories along the way.

Setting realistic training goals involves understanding your dog's capabilities and limitations. Take into account your dog's age, breed, temperament, and previous training experience when setting your training goals.

The goal of training is not to have a perfect dog, but to build a strong, trusting relationship with your dog. It's about understanding and communication. It's about raising a happy, well-behaved dog who is a joy to live with.

In conclusion, training is an essential part of your dog's life. It provides structure, prevents behavioral problems, enhances safety, and strengthens the bond between you and your dog. With patience, consistency, and positive reinforcement, you can train your dog effectively and enjoy a rewarding, fulfilling relationship with them. So let's embark on this training journey together, and let's raise happy, well-behaved dogs.

How Dogs Learn: The Basics of Positive Reinforcement

As we delve deeper into the world of dog training, it's important to understand the fundamental principle that underpins effective training: positive reinforcement. This principle is based on the simple yet powerful concept that behaviors followed by pleasant outcomes are likely to be repeated.

Understanding how dogs learn through positive reinforcement begins with a basic appreciation of their cognitive abilities. Dogs, like many other animals, learn from their experiences. They make connections between their actions and the consequences of those actions. If an action leads to a positive outcome, they are likely to repeat it. If it leads to a negative outcome, they are likely to avoid it in the future. This is the essence of learning through positive reinforcement.

Imagine you're teaching your dog to sit. You say the command "sit," and your dog, perhaps a little confused at first, eventually sits down. You immediately reward them with a treat and lots of praise. Your dog enjoys the treat and the attention, associating these positive experiences with the act of sitting on command. Over time, your dog learns that sitting when you say "sit" leads to good things, so they continue to do it.

Positive reinforcement is not just about giving treats, though. It's about rewarding any behavior you want to encourage, whether it's sitting, staying, coming when called, or even just being calm and relaxed. The reward can be anything your dog finds enjoyable: a favorite toy, a belly rub, a game of fetch, or just a kind word and a pat on the head.

One of the key advantages of positive reinforcement is that it fosters a positive relationship between you and your dog. It's a method based on mutual respect and understanding. It allows you to communicate with your dog in a way that's clear, kind, and effective. It makes training an enjoyable experience for your dog, which can significantly speed up the learning process.

However, for positive reinforcement to work, timing is crucial. Dogs live in the moment. They don't have the ability to connect an action with a consequence unless the two are closely linked in time. This means that you need to reward your dog immediately after they perform the desired behavior. Even a delay of a few seconds can make it difficult for your dog to make the connection.

Consistency is another key factor in positive reinforcement training. Dogs thrive on consistency. They learn best when the rules are clear and unchanging. If you reward your dog for a behavior one day and ignore it the next, your dog will be confused and unsure of what you want. Make sure to reward your dog every time they perform the desired behavior, especially in the early stages of training.

It's also important to note that positive reinforcement is about rewarding good behavior, not punishing bad behavior. Punishment can be confusing and frightening for dogs. It can damage your relationship with your dog and lead to fear, anxiety, and even aggression. Instead of punishing your dog for what they've done wrong, focus on teaching them what you want them to do and rewarding them when they do it.

Positive reinforcement is a powerful tool in dog training, but it's not a magic wand. It requires patience, consistency, and a good understanding of your dog's needs and motivations. It's a process, a journey you embark on with your dog. There will be challenges along the way, but the rewards—a well-behaved dog, a strong bond, and a harmonious home—are well worth the effort.

As you navigate the world of dog training, remember: you are your dog's guide, their teacher, their trusted leader. Your job is not to control your dog, but to help them understand the world around them. To show them what's expected of them, to guide them towards good behavior, and to reward them for their efforts. With positive reinforcement, patience, and love, you can help your dog become the best they can be.

Setting Realistic Training Goals

As you embark on the journey of training your dog, it's crucial to set realistic training goals. These goals will guide your training sessions, provide a measure of progress, and help keep both you and your dog motivated. However, it's important to remember that every dog is unique, and their learning pace and abilities can vary greatly. Setting realistic training goals requires understanding your dog's individual capabilities, temperament, and learning style.

When we talk about setting realistic training goals, we're not talking about expecting your dog to perform complex tricks or behave perfectly all the time. Rather, we're talking about setting achievable milestones that contribute to your dog's overall behavior, well-being, and your mutual understanding.

For example, a realistic training goal for a new puppy might be learning to respond to their name or mastering the "sit" command. For an older dog with no previous training, a realistic goal might be learning to walk on a leash without pulling. These are simple, achievable goals that contribute to your dog's overall behavior and obedience.

When setting training goals, it's important to consider your dog's age, breed, and previous training experience. Puppies have shorter attention spans than adult dogs and might require shorter, more frequent training sessions. Certain breeds are known for their intelligence and eagerness to please and may pick up on new commands more quickly, while others may require a bit more patience and repetition.

Your dog's previous training experience will also play a significant role in setting training goals. A dog with no previous training or a history of negative experiences with training may require more time and patience to learn new behaviors. On the other hand, a dog with positive training experiences may be more eager to learn and quicker to pick up on new commands.

Training is not a race, and there's no set timeline for when your dog should learn certain behaviors. What's important is consistency, patience, and positive reinforcement. Celebrate small victories along the way, and don't get discouraged if progress seems slow. Training is as much about the journey as it is about the destination.

It's also important to be flexible with your training goals. If a certain technique isn't working, or if your dog is struggling to master a particular command, don't be afraid to adjust your goals or try a different approach. The goal of training is to enhance your relationship with your dog and improve their behavior, not to adhere rigidly to a set plan.

Moreover, setting realistic training goals is not a one-time task. As your dog masters certain behaviors, new goals will naturally arise. Perhaps your dog has mastered basic commands and you're ready to move on to more advanced training. Or maybe your dog has shown an aptitude for a particular task or trick that you'd like to further develop.

Setting realistic training goals is a crucial part of effective dog training. By understanding your dog's unique capabilities and learning style, you can set goals that are challenging, achievable, and tailored to your dog's needs. Remember, the goal of training is not perfection, but progress. With patience, consistency, and positive reinforcement, you and your dog can enjoy the rewarding journey of training together.

So, as you embark on this training journey, remember to set realistic goals, celebrate small victories, and always keep the lines of communication open with your dog. Training is a journey, and every step forward, no matter how small, is a step in the right direction. Here's to a rewarding and successful training journey with your furry friend.

Chapter 1

PREPARING YOUR HOME FOR A NEW DOG

Puppy-Proofing Essentials

Imagine the excitement and anticipation of bringing home a new puppy. The joy of their first wagging tail, the softness of their fur, the adorable way they tilt their head when they're trying to understand something. But before you can enjoy these precious moments, there's an important task you need to undertake - puppy-proofing your home.

Puppy-proofing is a crucial step in preparing your home for a new dog. It's about creating a safe environment where your puppy can explore, learn, and grow. Puppies are naturally curious and love to explore their surroundings. This curiosity, while essential for their learning and development, can also lead them into potentially dangerous situations. That's where puppy-proofing comes in.

Think of puppy-proofing as baby-proofing for your new furry family member. It involves looking at your home from your puppy's perspective and identifying potential hazards. Begin by getting down on your hands and knees to see the world from your puppy's viewpoint. This will help you spot potential dangers that you might not notice from your regular height.

One of the first things you'll notice is that puppies love to chew. Whether it's due to teething or just plain curiosity, puppies will chew on just about anything they can get their paws on. Electrical cords, shoes, furniture, and small objects can all pose a risk to your puppy. Secure electrical cords out of reach, keep shoes and other chewable items in closed closets or high shelves, and ensure small objects are not left on the floor.

Next, consider areas or items in your home that could potentially harm your puppy. This includes cleaning supplies, medications, certain plants, and even some human foods. Install child-proof locks on cabinets that contain harmful substances, and keep your trash can secure. If you have plants, do some research to ensure they're not toxic to dogs. If they are, move them to a place where your puppy can't reach them.

Don't forget about the outside. If you have a yard where your puppy will be playing, make sure it's secure. Check the fence for any gaps your puppy could squeeze through. Remove any toxic plants, secure trash cans, and make sure there are no small objects your puppy could swallow.

While it's important to make your home safe for your puppy, it's equally important to make it comfortable. Create a designated space for your puppy with a comfortable bed and plenty of toys. This will give your puppy a sense of security and help with training and housebreaking.

Remember, puppy-proofing is an ongoing process. As your puppy grows and learns, new risks may emerge. Regularly reassess your home for potential hazards and adjust as necessary.

Puppy-proofing is an essential step in preparing your home for a new dog. It's about creating a safe, welcoming environment where your puppy can learn and grow. By taking the time to properly puppy-proof your home, you're setting the stage for a smooth transition and a happy, healthy life for your new furry friend. So, before you bring your new puppy home, take the time to puppy-proof your home. Your puppy (and your shoes and furniture) will thank you.

Creating a Welcoming Environment

Creating a welcoming environment for your new dog is as crucial as puppy-proofing your home. It's about making your dog feel safe, comfortable, and loved from the moment they step paw into their new home. A welcoming environment can help ease the transition for your new pet and set the stage for a successful bonding and training process.

Firstly, consider where your dog will spend most of their time. This space should be safe, comfortable, and free from potential hazards. It should be a space where your dog can relax, play, and sleep. Consider providing a cozy bed, a few toys, and easy access to food and water. If you're bringing home a puppy or a dog that's not yet house-trained, make sure this area is easy to clean.

Next, think about the noise level in your home. Dogs, especially new ones, can be easily startled by loud noises. Try to keep the noise level down for the first few days to allow your dog to adjust to their new environment. If you live in a noisy area or have loud household members, consider using white noise machines or soft music to help drown out the noise.

Lighting is another important factor to consider. Just like humans, dogs can be scared of the dark. Leaving a light on for your dog at night can help them feel more secure. On the other hand, bright, harsh lighting can be stressful for dogs. Use natural light whenever possible and avoid using bright, overhead lights.

One of the most important aspects of creating a welcoming environment for your dog is providing plenty of opportunities for enrichment. This includes toys, puzzles, and plenty of opportunities for exercise. Regular play and exercise will not only help keep your dog physically healthy but also mentally stimulated.

Creating a welcoming environment also means establishing a routine as soon as possible. Dogs thrive on routine as it gives them a sense of security and helps them understand what's expected of them. Try to feed, walk, and play with your dog at the same times each day. This will help your dog adjust more quickly to their new home and can also aid in training and housebreaking.

Every dog is unique and what feels welcoming to one dog might not feel the same to another. Pay attention to your dog's reactions to different environments and adjust accordingly. If your dog seems uncomfortable or scared, try to identify the cause and make the necessary changes.

Finally, the most important part of creating a welcoming environment for your new dog is you. Your attitude, behavior, and emotions can greatly affect how your dog feels in their new home. Try to remain calm and patient as your dog adjusts to their new surroundings. Spend plenty of time with your dog, engaging in positive interactions like playing, grooming, and training.

In conclusion, creating a welcoming environment for your new dog involves considering their physical comfort, mental stimulation, and emotional well-being. By providing a safe, comfortable space, establishing a routine, and engaging in positive interactions, you can help your new dog feel at home. Remember, the goal is not to create a perfect environment, but to create an environment where your dog feels safe, loved, and at home. With patience, empathy, and a little planning, you can create a welcoming environment for your new furry friend.

Gathering the Right Supplies

Bringing a new dog home is an exciting time filled with joy, anticipation, and, of course, preparation. One of the key steps in preparing for your new furry friend's arrival is gathering the right supplies. From food and water bowls to toys and grooming tools, having the right supplies on hand will make the transition smoother for both you and your dog.

First and foremost, your dog will need high-quality dog food. The type of food you choose will depend on your dog's age, breed, size, and health status. Puppies generally require food that's specially formulated for their growth and development, while adult dogs need food that's suited to their size and activity level. Always consult with a vet to determine the best diet for your dog.

Next, you'll need bowls for food and water. Stainless steel or ceramic bowls are generally the best choices as they're durable, easy to clean, and resistant to bacteria. Avoid plastic bowls as they can harbor bacteria and cause allergic reactions in some dogs.

A comfortable bed is another must-have. Dogs, just like humans, need a comfortable place to rest and sleep. The bed should be large enough for your dog to stretch out comfortably, but cozy enough to make them feel secure. Consider the bed's material and ensure it's durable, washable, and suitable for your dog's breed and size.

Collars, leashes, and identification tags are also essential. A collar should fit comfortably, allowing for two fingers to slip easily between the collar and your dog's neck. The leash should be sturdy and appropriate for your dog's size. An identification tag, which can be attached to the collar, should include your contact information to ensure your dog can be returned to you if they get lost.

Toys are crucial for your dog's mental stimulation and physical exercise. They come in all shapes and sizes - from chew toys that can help with teething in puppies to puzzle toys that challenge your dog's mind. Ensure the toys are safe for your dog, with no small parts they could choke on.

Grooming supplies are another important category. Depending on your dog's breed and coat type, you might need a brush or comb, dog shampoo, nail clippers, and possibly even dental care products.

Regular grooming not only keeps your dog looking their best but also provides an opportunity to check for any skin issues or parasites.

Training supplies, such as treats and possibly a crate, will also be needed. Treats are a great tool for positive reinforcement training, while a crate can be a safe, comforting space for your dog if used correctly.

Lastly, don't forget about health supplies. A first-aid kit for dogs is a must-have for any pet owner. It should include items like bandages, tweezers, a digital thermometer, and a list of emergency contact numbers, including your vet's.

These are just the basics. The specific supplies you'll need may vary based on your dog's breed, age, size, and individual needs. For example, puppies may require puppy pads for house training, while older dogs might benefit from orthopedic beds.

Gathering the right supplies is a crucial step in preparing for a new dog. It ensures you're ready to provide for your dog's physical, mental, and emotional needs from the moment they arrive. By preparing in advance, you can focus on what truly matters when your new pet arrives - building a bond and starting your journey together.

Planning Feeding, Sleeping, and Play Areas

As you prepare your home for the arrival of your new dog, one of the most important steps is planning their feeding, sleeping, and play areas. These areas are essential for your dog's well-being and will play a significant role in their adjustment to their new home.

Let's start with the feeding area. This should be a quiet, low-traffic area where your dog can eat without distractions or interruptions. It's important to choose a place where you can easily clean up any spills, so a hard, non-carpeted floor is ideal. Keep the feeding area consistent, as changing it can cause confusion and stress for your dog. Also, remember to place fresh water in this area and replenish it regularly.

Next is the sleeping area. This should be a comfortable, cozy space where your dog can rest undisturbed. It could be a dog bed in the corner of a room, a crate if crate training, or even a designated piece of furniture, depending on your house rules. The sleeping area should be away from drafts and not too close to heating sources. It's also a good idea to place it somewhere where your dog can see you, as this can provide them with a sense of security and comfort.

The play area is where your dog will spend a lot of their time, especially if you're bringing home a puppy. This area should be spacious enough for your dog to move around freely and safely. Make sure it's free from any objects that could be knocked over or any items that could pose a choking hazard. It's also important to ensure that this area is easy to supervise, as you'll need to keep an eye on your dog while they're playing, especially in the early days.

If you have a yard, it can serve as an excellent play area for your dog. However, you'll need to ensure it's secure to prevent your dog from escaping. Check for any gaps in fences and ensure gates are secure. Also, remove any toxic plants or garden chemicals that could harm your dog.

When planning these areas, remember to consider your dog's size, breed, and age. A larger breed will need more space to move around than a smaller one. Puppies may need a more contained play area to keep them safe, while older dogs might appreciate a quieter, more comfortable sleeping area.

Consistency is key when planning these areas. Dogs thrive on routine and consistency, so try to keep these areas as constant as possible. This can help your dog feel more secure and help with training and behavior.

Lastly, involve all family members in the planning process. Everyone should know where the feeding, sleeping, and play areas are and the rules associated with each. This can help ensure consistency and make the transition smoother for your dog.

Planning your dog's feeding, sleeping, and play areas is a crucial step in preparing your home for a new dog. These areas will play a significant role in your dog's life and their adjustment to their new home. By carefully planning these spaces, you can help ensure your dog's comfort, safety, and happiness in their new environment. So take the time to plan these areas carefully - your new furry friend will thank you for it.

Preparing the Family

Preparing your family for the arrival of a new dog is just as important as preparing your home. The addition of a new pet is a significant event that can affect everyone in the household. It's essential to ensure that all family members understand the responsibilities that come with pet ownership and are ready to contribute to the dog's care and training.

Begin by discussing the responsibilities that come with having a dog. This includes feeding, walking, grooming, and training the dog, as well as taking them to vet appointments. Depending on the age and maturity of your children, they can take on some of these responsibilities. This can help them feel involved and teach them valuable lessons about responsibility and empathy.

Next, set clear rules about how to interact with the dog. This includes how to handle the dog, when to play with the dog, and what behaviors are not acceptable. For example, pulling the dog's tail or ears, bothering the dog while they're eating or sleeping, or teasing the dog are all behaviors that should be off-limits. It's important for everyone to understand that dogs, like people, need respect and personal space.

It's also essential to discuss the importance of consistency in training. Dogs learn through repetition and consistency, so it's crucial that all family members use the same commands and follow the same rules. This can prevent confusion for the dog and make the training process smoother and more effective.

If your family has never had a dog before, consider doing some research together. Read books about dog care and training, watch educational videos, or even attend a pet care workshop. This can help everyone understand what to expect and how to care for a new dog.

Finally, prepare your family for the changes that a new dog will bring. This might include waking up earlier for morning walks, spending more time at home, or even dealing with some initial behavior issues as the dog adjusts to their new home. It's important to remember that while having a dog can be rewarding and fun, it also requires commitment and patience.

Preparing your family for a new dog is a crucial step in the process of bringing a new pet into your home. By discussing responsibilities, setting clear rules, and learning about dog care and training together, you can ensure that everyone is ready for the arrival of your new furry friend. A dog is not just a pet, but a new member of the family. With preparation, understanding, and love, your family can provide a happy and welcoming home for your new dog.

Chapter 2

UNDERSTANDING YOUR DOG'S DEVELOPMENT

Puppy Developmental Stages

Understanding your puppy's developmental stages is crucial to providing them with the care, training, and socialization they need to grow into a well-adjusted adult dog. A puppy's first year is filled with rapid growth and development, and being aware of these stages can help you navigate the joys and challenges of puppyhood.

The first stage of puppy development begins at birth and lasts until about two weeks of age. This is known as the neonatal period. During this time, puppies are entirely dependent on their mother. Their eyes and ears are closed, and they spend most of their time eating and sleeping. Despite their limited interaction with the world, this is a crucial time for their development.

Next comes the transitional period, which typically occurs between two and four weeks of age. During this stage, puppies start to open their eyes and ears and begin to explore their surroundings. They start to stand, walk, and even wag their tails. This is also when they begin to interact with their littermates, learning the basics of dog communication.

The socialization period, from four to twelve weeks, is perhaps the most critical stage in a puppy's development. During this time, puppies are extremely impressionable and their experiences can have a lasting impact on their behavior. It's crucial to expose puppies to a variety of people, environments, and other animals during this stage to help them grow into confident, well-socialized dogs.

From twelve weeks to six months, puppies enter the juvenile stage. This is when they start to test boundaries and explore their independence, much like human teenagers. They may become more energetic and possibly more challenging to manage. Consistent training and positive reinforcement are crucial during this stage.

The adolescent stage, from six months to two years, is when puppies reach sexual maturity. This can be a challenging time for dog owners as dogs may start to display new behaviors, such as marking or mounting. They may also become more independent and less focused on pleasing their owners. Again, consistency and patience in training are key during this stage.

Understanding these stages can help you provide your puppy with the appropriate care, training, and socialization. Remember, every puppy is unique and may progress through these stages at their own pace. Some may need more time and patience, while others may breeze through certain stages.

Understanding your puppy's developmental stages is an essential part of raising a happy, healthy, and well-behaved dog. By knowing what to expect at each stage, you can better meet your puppy's needs and help guide them through the exciting journey of growing up. After all, raising a puppy is not just about training them, but also about understanding them and helping them navigate the world.

Teenage Years and Training Challenges

The teenage years in a dog's life, typically from six months to two years, can be a challenging time for both the dog and the owner. This is a period of significant physical and behavioral changes, often marked by increased independence and a testing of boundaries. Understanding these changes and the associated training challenges can help you navigate this phase more effectively.

During the teenage phase, your dog is essentially an adolescent. They're no longer a puppy, but they're not quite an adult yet. This is the time when your dog will reach sexual maturity, which can lead to new behaviors such as marking, mounting, or even aggression in some cases. Female dogs will have their first heat cycle, while male dogs may start to show interest in females.

One of the biggest challenges during this stage is dealing with a sudden change in behavior. Your previously obedient puppy might start ignoring commands, become easily distracted, or start to push boundaries. This is often because their world is expanding and becoming more exciting, and they're testing their independence.

This can be frustrating for dog owners, but it's important to remember that this is a normal part of your dog's development.

Patience, consistency, and positive reinforcement are key during this stage. Continue with your training routines, even if it seems like your dog is forgetting everything they've learned. They're not - they're just more interested in exploring their world.

Socialization continues to be important during the teenage years. Continue to expose your dog to a variety of people, environments, and other animals to help them become well-rounded adults. However, be mindful of their increased sensitivity to negative experiences. Negative encounters during this stage can have a lasting impact, so it's important to ensure all interactions are positive.

Physical exercise and mental stimulation are also crucial during the teenage years. Your dog will have a lot of energy, and providing outlets for that energy can help prevent destructive behaviors. Regular walks, playtime, and training sessions can help keep your dog physically active and mentally stimulated.

Finally, remember to provide plenty of love and positive reinforcement. Even though your dog is growing up, they still need your love and approval. Praise them for good behavior, spend quality time with them, and show them that you're there for them, even when they're pushing boundaries.

The teenage years can be a challenging time in a dog's life, but with understanding, patience, and consistent training, you can guide your dog through this phase. Remember, your dog is learning and growing, just like a human teenager. With your support and guidance, they can navigate the challenges of adolescence and grow into a well-behaved, confident adult.

Training Older Dogs: Starting Fresh

Training older dogs, whether they're newly adopted or long-time family members, can be a rewarding experience. While it's true that older dogs may come with ingrained behaviors or habits, it's also true that they can learn new things. Starting fresh with an older dog might require patience and understanding, but with the right approach, you can teach an old dog new tricks.

One of the biggest advantages of training older dogs is that they often have longer attention spans than puppies. This can make them more receptive to training sessions. However, it's important to keep training sessions short and sweet to prevent fatigue and keep your dog engaged. Aim for 15-minute sessions a few times a day.

Before you begin training an older dog, it's essential to understand their history. If they're a rescue or adopted dog, they may have had experiences that could affect their behavior or their ability to learn certain commands. For instance, a dog that was punished for sitting in a previous home might be hesitant to learn the "sit" command. Understanding these nuances can help you tailor your training approach.

Positive reinforcement is the key to training dogs of all ages, but it's especially crucial for older dogs. This method of training rewards good behavior, which encourages your dog to repeat it. Rewards can be treats, toys, praise, or anything else your dog loves. Remember to reward your dog immediately after they perform the desired behavior to help them make the connection.

Patience is another essential factor when training older dogs. Some may learn new commands or behaviors quickly, while others may need more time. It's important not to rush the process. Allow your dog to learn at their own pace, offering plenty of encouragement along the way.

Consistency is also crucial. Make sure everyone in your household is using the same commands and rewards to avoid confusing your dog. If you're teaching your dog not to jump on people, for example, everyone in the family needs to reinforce this rule.

It's also important to consider your older dog's physical health. Older dogs may have health issues that could affect their ability to perform certain commands. Arthritis, for instance, might make it difficult for a dog to sit or lie down on command. Always consult with a vet before starting a training program and modify commands as necessary to accommodate your dog's physical abilities.

Lastly, remember that training should be a positive experience for both you and your dog. It's a chance to spend quality time together and strengthen your bond. Keep training sessions upbeat and end on a positive note to keep your dog looking forward to the next session.

Training older dogs and starting fresh can be a rewarding experience. While it may require patience and understanding, with positive reinforcement, consistency, and a consideration for your dog's past and physical health, you can teach your old dog new tricks. Remember, the goal of training isn't just to have a well-behaved dog, but also to enhance your relationship with your dog. With patience, love, and consistency, you can make the golden years of your dog's life the best they can be.

Understanding Dog Body Language

Understanding your dog's body language is a vital part of building a strong, trusting relationship with your pet. Dogs communicate primarily through body language, and being able to interpret these signals can enhance your bond with your dog and help prevent misunderstandings or potential conflicts.

One of the most expressive parts of a dog's body is their tail. A wagging tail is often associated with happiness, but the speed, direction, and position of the wag can convey different emotions. For instance, a high, stiff wag can indicate excitement or agitation, while a slow, relaxed wag generally signals a relaxed and content dog. A tail tucked between the legs often signifies fear or submission.

Ears are another key indicator of a dog's mood. Erect ears typically indicate that a dog is alert and attentive, while ears that are laid back can signal fear, aggression, or submission, depending on the situation. It's important to consider the natural position of your dog's ears, as different breeds have different ear shapes and positions.

A dog's eyes can also reveal a lot about their emotional state. Soft, relaxed eyes usually mean a dog is calm and content, while wide, alert eyes can indicate excitement or fear. If a dog avoids eye contact, it can be a sign of submission or discomfort. Conversely, a direct, prolonged stare can be a sign of aggression.

The position and movement of a dog's body also provide clues to their feelings. A relaxed body usually means a dog is comfortable, while a stiff body can indicate tension or discomfort. A dog that's leaning forward is likely feeling confident and may be ready to play, while a dog leaning away or turning their body sideways might be anxious or fearful.

The way a dog uses their mouth can also communicate different emotions. A relaxed, open mouth usually indicates a relaxed and happy dog. Yawning can signal stress or tiredness, while lip licking or showing the whites of their eyes (known as whale eye) can indicate anxiety or stress.

However, it's important to remember that body language can vary between individual dogs, and what's normal for one dog might not be normal for another. It's also crucial to consider the context. For instance, a dog that's baring their teeth might be aggressive, or they might simply be panting heavily after exercise.

Understanding your dog's body language takes time and observation. Spend time watching your dog in different situations - when they're relaxed at home, out on walks, meeting new people or dogs. Over time, you'll start to understand their unique ways of expressing themselves.

Understanding your dog's body language is a key part of building a strong, trusting relationship with your pet. By paying attention to your dog's tail, ears, eyes, body, and mouth, you can gain valuable insights into their emotional state and better respond to their needs. Remember, every dog is unique, and understanding your dog's individual body language is part of the joy of getting to know your furry friend.

Building a Bond and Trust

Building a bond and trust with your dog is one of the most rewarding aspects of dog ownership. This bond is the foundation of a strong, healthy relationship between you and your pet. It enhances communication, makes training easier, and ultimately leads to a happier and more fulfilling life for both of you.

One of the most effective ways to build a bond with your dog is through spending quality time together. This can be as simple as a daily walk, playtime in the yard, or just relaxing together at home. These shared experiences not only provide your dog with physical exercise and mental stimulation, but they also give you both the opportunity to enjoy each other's company and build a stronger connection.

Training is another powerful tool for building trust and bonding with your dog. Training sessions provide an opportunity for you to communicate clearly with your dog, and for your dog to learn to understand and respond to you. Remember to always use positive reinforcement methods in training. Rewarding your dog for good behavior, rather than punishing them for bad behavior, builds trust and encourages them to see you as a source of good things.

Consistency is also key in building trust. Dogs thrive on routine and predictability. By being consistent in your interactions with your dog, you help them understand what to expect from you, which can greatly enhance their trust in you.

Respecting your dog's needs and feelings is another crucial aspect of building trust. This means recognizing when your dog is scared, anxious, or uncomfortable, and responding in a way that makes them feel safe and understood. It also means respecting their need for personal space and alone time.

Finally, remember that building a bond and trust with your dog is a process that takes time. It can't be rushed. Be patient with your dog, and with yourself. Celebrate the small victories and progress you make together, and don't get discouraged by setbacks.

Building a bond and trust with your dog is a journey that requires time, patience, and understanding. By spending quality time with your dog, training them with positive reinforcement, being consistent, and respecting their needs and feelings, you can build a strong, trusting relationship that enhances both your lives. Remember, the bond you share with your dog is unique and special, and nurturing it is one of the greatest joys of dog ownership.

Chapter 3

CRATE TRAINING AND SAFE SPACES

Benefits of Crate Training

Crate training is a method that uses a dog's natural instincts as a den animal, and when done correctly, it can have numerous benefits for both you and your dog. While some people may initially feel uncomfortable with the idea of crate training, it's important to remember that a crate is not a cage, but rather a safe and comfortable space for your dog.

One of the primary benefits of crate training is that it can be a highly effective tool for house training. Dogs naturally avoid soiling their den, and a crate can help teach your dog to control their bladder and bowels. By establishing a routine where your dog spends short periods in the crate and is then taken outside to eliminate, you can help them learn when and where they should do their business.

Crate training can also provide your dog with a sense of security and comfort. Dogs, like their wolf ancestors, are den animals and can find comfort in having a space of their own. A crate can serve as your dog's personal den, a place where they can retreat to when they need rest or when they're feeling overwhelmed. This can be especially beneficial during times of change or stress, such as during a move or a loud holiday celebration.

Furthermore, a crate can keep your dog safe when you can't supervise them. This can be particularly useful with puppies or dogs that have a tendency to get into mischief when left alone. By keeping your dog in a crate, you can ensure they're not chewing on dangerous objects, getting into the trash, or engaging in other potentially harmful behaviors.

In addition to keeping your dog safe, crate training can also protect your belongings. Dogs, especially puppies, often go through a phase of chewing on anything they can get their paws on. A crate can keep your shoes, furniture, and other belongings safe from your dog's curious mouth.

Lastly, a crate can make travel safer and less stressful for your dog. Whether you're taking your dog on a road trip or to the vet, having them in a crate can keep them secure and calm. Many hotels and airlines also require dogs to be crate-trained for travel.

Crate training can offer numerous benefits, including aiding in house training, providing a safe and comfortable space for your dog, keeping your dog and your belongings safe, and making travel easier. It's important to remember that a crate should never be used as a form of punishment, and your dog should not be left in a crate for long periods of time. With patience, consistency, and positive reinforcement, a crate can become a positive aspect of your dog's life.

Choosing the Right Crate for Your Dog

Choosing the right crate for your dog is a critical step in the crate training process. The right crate can make your dog feel safe and secure, while the wrong crate can make them feel uncomfortable or anxious. There are several factors to consider when choosing a crate for your dog, including size, material, and design.

Size is perhaps the most important factor to consider. The crate should be large enough for your dog to stand up, turn around, and lie down comfortably. However, it should not be so large that your dog can eliminate at one end and sleep at the other. If you're crate training a puppy, consider getting a crate with a divider that can be adjusted as your puppy grows. This will allow you to keep the crate the appropriate size for your puppy at each stage of their growth.

The material of the crate is another important consideration. There are three main types of crates: wire crates, plastic crates, and soft-sided crates. Wire crates are durable and provide good ventilation. They often come with a removable tray for easy cleaning and a divider for adjusting the size. Plastic crates are lightweight and easy to clean. They can provide a more den-like feel, which some dogs may prefer. However, they offer less ventilation than wire crates. Soft-sided crates are lightweight and portable, making them a good choice for travel. However, they may not be durable enough for dogs that like to chew or scratch.

The design of the crate can also affect how comfortable your dog feels. Some dogs prefer a crate with more visibility, while others feel more secure in a crate with less visibility. If your dog is easily distracted or anxious, a crate with less visibility may be a better choice. On the other hand, if your dog likes to see what's going on around them, a crate with more visibility might be more suitable.

The location of the crate in your home can also impact your dog's comfort. The crate should be placed in a quiet, low-traffic area where your dog can relax without being disturbed. However, it should also be in an area where your dog can still feel part of the family. Many dogs like to be able to see their owners or other family members from their crate.

Finally, consider your dog's individual needs and preferences. Some dogs may prefer a certain type of crate over others. For example, a dog with anxiety might feel more secure in a plastic crate that provides more coverage, while a dog that gets hot easily might prefer a wire crate for better ventilation.

Choosing the right crate for your dog involves considering the size, material, design, and location of the crate, as well as your dog's individual needs and preferences. By taking the time to choose the right crate, you can make the crate training process smoother and more successful, and create a safe and comfortable space for your dog. Remember, the goal of crate training is to make the crate a positive place where your dog feels safe and secure. With the right crate, you can help achieve this goal and enhance your dog's overall well-being.

Starting Crate Training: Step-by-Step

Starting crate training with your dog can seem like a daunting task, but by breaking it down into manageable steps, it can be a smooth and rewarding process. The key to successful crate training is to make the crate a positive and comfortable place for your dog, and to progress at a pace that suits your dog's comfort level.

The first step in crate training is to introduce your dog to the crate. Place the crate in a common area of your home where your dog spends a lot of time. Leave the door open and let your dog explore the crate at their own pace. You can encourage exploration by placing treats or toys in the crate, but remember not to force your dog into the crate. The goal is for your dog to choose to enter the crate on their own.

Once your dog is comfortable entering the crate, you can start feeding them their meals in the crate. This creates a positive association with the crate. Start by placing the food near the entrance of the crate, and gradually move it further back over time. Once your dog is comfortable eating in the crate, you can start closing the door while they eat, opening it again as soon as they're finished. Gradually increase the amount of time the door stays closed after your dog has finished eating.

The next step is to start practicing short periods of confinement in the crate. Encourage your dog to enter the crate using a command such as "crate" or "bed", then close the door and stay nearby. Start with short periods of time, such as a few minutes, and gradually increase the duration. Always reward your dog for entering the crate and staying calm.

Once your dog is comfortable with short periods of confinement, you can start leaving them in the crate for longer periods while you're at home. This can help your dog learn that the crate is a safe place to relax, even when you're not right next to them. Remember to provide your dog with something to do in the crate, such as a chew toy or a puzzle toy filled with treats.

The final step is to start leaving your dog in the crate when you leave the house. Start with short absences and gradually increase the length of time you're gone. Always ensure your dog has been exercised and has had a chance to eliminate before you leave them in the crate.

Throughout the crate training process, it's important to remember to never use the crate as a punishment. The crate should always be a positive and safe place for your dog. If your dog seems anxious or distressed at any point, slow down and go back to the previous step.

Crate training is a gradual process that involves introducing your dog to the crate, feeding them in the crate, practicing short periods of confinement, leaving them in the crate while you're at home, and eventually leaving them in the crate when you're not home. By progressing at your dog's pace and maintaining a positive association with the crate, you can help your dog see the crate as a safe and comfortable place. Remember, patience and consistency are key in successful crate training. With time and practice, your dog can learn to love their crate, providing them with a safe space of their own.

Crate Training for Alone Time and Independence

Crate training can be an effective tool in teaching your dog to enjoy alone time and fostering independence. Dogs, like humans, need time to themselves to relax and recharge. A crate can provide a safe, comfortable space for your dog to enjoy this alone time.

When used correctly, a crate can help reduce separation anxiety in dogs. Many dogs feel anxious when left alone, but a crate can provide a secure, familiar environment that helps them feel safe. By associating the crate with positive experiences, such as meals, treats, and comfortable bedding, your dog can learn to see the crate as a relaxing place where good things happen.

To use crate training to promote alone time and independence, start by encouraging your dog to spend time in the crate while you're home. This can help your dog understand that the crate is not a place of isolation, but rather a place of comfort. You can do this by providing your dog with activities to enjoy in the crate, such as chew toys or puzzle toys filled with treats.

Once your dog is comfortable spending time in the crate while you're home, you can start leaving them in the crate for short periods while you're away. Start with short absences, such as running a quick errand, and gradually increase the length of time you're gone. Always ensure your dog has been exercised and has had a chance to eliminate before you leave them in the crate.

Remember to make your departures and arrivals low-key to avoid creating anxiety around these events. A calm goodbye can reassure your dog, while a calm hello can prevent overexcitement upon your return.

It's important to remember that a crate is not a solution for all dogs with separation anxiety or for all situations. Some dogs may feel more anxious in a crate, while others may need more than just a crate to feel comfortable when left alone. If your dog shows signs of distress when left in the crate, such as excessive barking, panting, or attempting to escape, it's important to seek advice from a professional dog trainer or a behaviorist.

Crate training can be a valuable tool in teaching your dog to enjoy alone time and fostering independence. By creating a positive association with the crate and gradually increasing the time your dog spends in the crate while you're away, you can help your dog feel safe and comfortable when left alone. Remember, every dog is unique, and what works for one dog may not work for another. Patience, understanding, and a willingness to adapt are key in successful crate training. With time and consistency, your dog can learn to see the crate as a safe, relaxing space, enhancing their comfort and independence.

Troubleshooting Common Issues

Crate training can be a smooth process for some dogs, but others may encounter a few bumps along the road. It's normal to face some challenges, and there are strategies to address common issues that arise during crate training.

One common issue is a dog who whines or barks in the crate. This can be a sign of distress or boredom. If your dog is barking or whining, first ensure their basic needs are met. Have they been fed, exercised, and given a chance to eliminate? If all these needs are met, they may need more time to adjust to the crate. Try providing a safe chew toy or a puzzle toy filled with treats to keep them occupied. If the whining or barking continues, it might be a sign of separation anxiety, and you may need to consult a professional.

Another issue is a dog who refuses to enter the crate. This can often be resolved by making the crate more appealing. Place your dog's favorite toys or treats in the crate, and use a cheerful voice to encourage them to enter. Never force your dog into the crate, as this can create a negative association. Patience and positive reinforcement are key.

A dog who soils the crate is another common issue. This can be a sign that your dog is being left in the crate for too long. Remember, puppies can only hold their bladder for one hour for every month of age, plus one. Adult dogs shouldn't be left in a crate for more than eight hours at a time. If your dog is soiling the crate despite appropriate crate times, it might be a sign of a medical issue, and you should consult your vet.

Finally, some dogs may chew on the crate or attempt to escape. This can be a sign of anxiety or boredom. Providing appropriate chew toys can help. If your dog is attempting to escape the crate, this can be a sign of distress, and you should seek advice from a professional.

While crate training can present some challenges, most can be addressed with patience, understanding, and a bit of creativity. Remember, the goal of crate training is to create a safe, comfortable space for your dog. If at any point the crate becomes a source of stress for your dog, it's important to take a step back and reassess your approach. With time and consistency, most dogs can learn to see the crate as a positive place, leading to a happier, more relaxed dog.

Chapter 4

POTTY TRAINING ESSENTIALS

Establishing a Routine

Establishing a routine is one of the most important steps in potty training your dog. Dogs are creatures of habit and thrive on consistency. A predictable schedule can help your dog understand when and where they are expected to eliminate, reducing the likelihood of accidents and making the potty training process smoother for both of you.

The first step in establishing a routine is to determine when your dog will need to go outside. This will largely depend on your dog's age and size. Puppies, for example, have small bladders and high metabolisms, which means they'll need to go out frequently. A good rule of thumb for puppies is to take them out every hour, as well as after meals, naps, and play sessions. Older dogs, on the other hand, may only need to go out three to five times a day.

Once you've determined how often your dog needs to go out, you can start to build a schedule. Try to take your dog out at the same times each day. For example, you might take your dog out first thing in the morning, after meals, and before bed. Consistency is key here. The more consistently you stick to the schedule, the quicker your dog will catch on.

In addition to scheduling potty breaks, it's also important to establish a routine for meals. Feeding your dog at the same times each day can help regulate their digestion and make their elimination more predictable. Avoid free feeding, where food is left out all day for your dog to graze. This can make it difficult to predict when your dog will need to go out and can slow down the potty training process.

When it's time for a potty break, take your dog to the same spot each time. This consistency can help your dog understand what is expected of them. Once at the spot, give your dog a command, such as "go potty," to help them associate the command with the action.

After your dog has done their business, it's important to return inside right away. This can help your dog understand that the purpose of the outing was to eliminate, not to play or explore. However, make sure to set aside separate times for walks and play so your dog gets plenty of exercise and mental stimulation.

Remember, establishing a routine takes time and patience. There will likely be a few accidents along the way, but that's a normal part of the process. Stay patient and consistent, and over time, your dog will start to understand the routine.

Establishing a routine is a crucial part of potty training. By determining how often your dog needs to go out, sticking to a consistent schedule, establishing a routine for meals, taking your dog to the same spot each time, and returning inside immediately after elimination, you can help your dog understand when and where they are expected to go. Remember, consistency is key in establishing a routine, and with time and patience, your dog will catch on.

Using Positive Reinforcement for Potty Training

Positive reinforcement is a powerful tool in potty training your dog. This training method involves rewarding your dog for desirable behavior, encouraging them to repeat that behavior in the future. When it comes to potty training, positive reinforcement can help your dog understand what is expected of them and motivate them to eliminate in the appropriate place.

The principle of positive reinforcement is simple: dogs will repeat behaviors that are rewarding. Therefore, by rewarding your dog for eliminating outside, you can encourage them to repeat this behavior. Rewards can come in many forms, including treats, praise, or playtime. The key is to find what motivates your dog the most and use that as a reward.

When your dog eliminates outside, it's important to reward them immediately. This immediate reinforcement helps your dog make the connection between the behavior (eliminating outside) and the reward. If you wait until you're back inside to reward your dog, they may not understand what they're being rewarded for.

In addition to rewarding your dog for eliminating outside, it's also important to reward them for signaling that they need to go out. Many dogs will show signs when they need to eliminate, such as sniffing, circling, or heading towards the door. By rewarding these signals, you can encourage your dog to communicate their needs clearly.

While positive reinforcement is about rewarding good behavior, it's equally important to avoid punishing your dog for accidents. Punishment can create fear and confusion, which can actually slow down the potty training process. If you catch your dog in the act of having an accident, simply interrupt them with a gentle "uh-oh" and take them outside. If you find an accident after the fact, just clean it up. Remember, accidents are a normal part of potty training and a sign that you need to adjust your routine or supervision.

It's also important to note that while treats can be a powerful motivator, they should be used judiciously. You don't want your dog to become dependent on treats for performing basic behaviors. As your dog becomes more consistent in eliminating outside, you can start to phase out treats, replacing them with praise or a quick game.

Positive reinforcement is a key component of potty training. By rewarding your dog for eliminating outside and for signaling their need to go out, you can encourage these behaviors. Remember to provide immediate reinforcement, avoid punishment for accidents, and use treats judiciously. With patience and consistency, positive reinforcement can make potty training a more enjoyable and successful experience for both you and your dog.

Recognizing Signals Your Dog Needs to Go

Recognizing the signals your dog gives when they need to eliminate is a crucial part of successful potty training. Dogs often display certain behaviors or changes in behavior when they need to go. Learning to read these signals can help you anticipate your dog's needs and prevent accidents before they happen.

One of the most common signals dogs give is a change in behavior. This could be anything from suddenly stopping what they're doing to pacing or circling. Some dogs might start sniffing the ground intensely, while others might head towards the door or try to get your attention in other ways. These behaviors can be subtle, especially in puppies, so it's important to keep a close eye on your dog, particularly during the potty training phase.

Another signal that your dog needs to go is a change in body language. This could include restlessness, squatting, or lifting a leg. Some dogs might whine or bark, while others might start scratching at the door. Again, these signals can be subtle and can vary from dog to dog, so it's important to learn what's normal for your dog and to watch for any changes in their behavior or body language.

Timing can also be a useful indicator. Most dogs need to eliminate when they wake up, after they eat, and after they play or exercise. By taking your dog out at these times, you can often prevent accidents before they happen. Additionally, puppies generally need to go out every hour, as well as after meals and naps. Keeping track of when your dog eliminates can help you predict when they'll need to go out.

While these signals can be helpful, it's important to remember that every dog is unique. It's crucial to spend time with your dog and get to know their individual habits and signals. This not only aids in potty training, but also strengthens your bond with your dog and improves overall communication.

If you're having trouble recognizing your dog's signals, don't despair. Some dogs are more subtle than others, and it can take time to learn their specific cues. Consistency, observation, and patience are key. And remember, accidents are a normal part of potty training and a sign that adjustments may need to be made in your routine or supervision.

Recognizing the signals your dog gives when they need to eliminate is a key part of successful potty training. By watching for changes in behavior and body language, and by understanding the timing of when your dog is likely to need to go, you can anticipate their needs and prevent accidents. Remember, every dog is unique, and patience and observation are key in learning your dog's specific signals. With time and consistency, you'll become an expert in reading your dog's signals, making the potty training process smoother and more successful for both of you.

Handling Accidents with Patience

Accidents are an inevitable part of the potty training process. Even the most diligent dog owner and the most intelligent dog will face a few mishaps along the way. The key to handling these accidents is patience. Reacting with frustration or anger will not speed up the process; in fact, it may even set your dog back. Understanding this and approaching accidents with a calm, patient attitude can make the potty training process smoother for both you and your dog.

When an accident happens, it's important to remember that your dog is not doing it out of spite or stubbornness. Dogs don't understand the concept of indoor versus outdoor bathroom etiquette until we teach them. If your dog has an accident, it's usually because they couldn't hold it any longer, didn't understand they were supposed to go outside, or didn't know how to tell you they needed to go out.

If you catch your dog in the act of having an accident, resist the urge to scold or punish them. Instead, interrupt them with a gentle "uh-oh" or a clap of your hands, and then immediately take them outside. If they finish eliminating outside, reward them with praise and a treat. This can help your dog make the connection that outside is the appropriate place to eliminate.

If you find an accident after the fact, simply clean it up. Scolding your dog after the fact won't help, as they won't make the connection between their earlier action and your current displeasure. Instead, use it as a learning opportunity. Think about why the accident might have happened. Were there too many hours between bathroom breaks? Did you ignore or miss a signal that your dog needed to go out? Use this information to adjust your routine and prevent future accidents.

Cleaning up accidents properly is also important. Dog urine contains pheromones that signal to your dog that this is an acceptable place to eliminate. Simply wiping up the mess won't remove these pheromones. Use an enzymatic cleaner specifically designed for pet messes to thoroughly clean the area and remove these pheromones.

Remember, patience is key. Potty training is a learning process, and like any learning process, it takes time and involves a few mistakes.

Keep your expectations realistic and celebrate small victories along the way. Your dog is doing their best to understand and follow your rules, and your patience, understanding, and consistency can help them achieve this.

Handling accidents with patience is a crucial part of the potty training process. By reacting calmly to accidents, using them as learning opportunities, and cleaning up thoroughly, you can help guide your dog towards successful potty training. Remember, every accident is a chance to learn and adjust your routine. With time, patience, and consistency, your dog will learn to navigate the rules of indoor living, leading to fewer accidents and a happier home for both of you.

Troubleshooting Potty Training Problems

Potty training a dog is not always a straightforward process. Sometimes, despite your best efforts, problems can arise that make the process more challenging. However, with a little troubleshooting, you can overcome these hurdles and guide your dog towards successful potty training.

One common problem is a dog that seems to have accidents frequently, even when taken out regularly. This could be a sign of a medical issue, such as a urinary tract infection or gastrointestinal upset. If your dog is having frequent accidents, it's worth a visit to the vet to rule out any underlying health problems.

Another common issue is regression, where a dog that seemed to be potty trained starts having accidents again. This can be frustrating, but it's important to remember that it's a common part of the training process. Regression can be caused by a variety of factors, including changes in the household, stress, or even just a lapse in supervision. When regression occurs, it's best to go back to basics. Reinstate the potty training routine you used initially, and be patient. With time and consistency, your dog will get back on track.

Sometimes, a dog may seem to prefer eliminating indoors, even when given frequent opportunities to go outside. This can often be resolved by making the outside more appealing and the inside less so. Spend more time outside with your dog, playing and having fun, so they form positive associations with being outside. At the same time, make sure to clean any indoor accident spots thoroughly with an enzymatic cleaner, to remove the scent that can draw your dog back to those spots.

A dog that eliminates in their crate can be a particularly challenging problem. This can be a sign that the crate is too large. Dogs naturally avoid soiling their sleeping area, but if the crate is too big, your dog may designate a portion of it as a bathroom. Make sure the crate is just large enough for your dog to stand, turn around, and lie down comfortably. If your dog continues to soil the crate, it could be a sign of a medical issue or separation anxiety, and it's worth consulting a professional.

Finally, remember that every dog is unique, and what works for one may not work for another. Patience, consistency, and a willingness to adapt your approach are key in troubleshooting potty training problems. And remember, it's okay to ask for help. If you're struggling with potty training, don't hesitate to reach out to a professional dog trainer or behaviorist. They can provide guidance and strategies tailored to your dog's specific needs and challenges.

While potty training problems can be frustrating, they are usually solvable with some troubleshooting. Whether it's frequent accidents, regression, a preference for eliminating indoors, or soiling the crate, these issues can often be addressed with a combination of medical intervention, routine adjustments, crate sizing, and professional help. With patience and persistence, you and your dog can overcome these hurdles and achieve successful potty training.

Chapter 5

THE POWER OF POSITIVE REINFORCEMENT

Basics of Positive Reinforcement

Positive reinforcement is a powerful and effective method for training dogs. It is based on the simple principle that behaviors that are rewarded are more likely to be repeated. In contrast to punishment-based methods, which focus on correcting unwanted behaviors, positive reinforcement emphasizes the importance of encouraging and rewarding desirable behaviors.

The concept of positive reinforcement is rooted in the science of animal behavior. When a dog performs a behavior that leads to a positive outcome, they are more likely to repeat that behavior in the future. For example, if your dog sits on command and is then rewarded with a treat, they will be more likely to sit on command in the future.

Rewards in positive reinforcement training can take many forms. Food treats are often used because they are a powerful motivator for most dogs. However, rewards can also include praise, petting, playtime, or anything else your dog enjoys. The key is to find what motivates your dog and use that as a reward.

To implement positive reinforcement, start by clearly deciding on the behavior you want to encourage. Then, wait for your dog to perform that behavior, or guide them towards it. As soon as they perform the desired behavior, immediately reward them. This immediate reinforcement helps your dog make the connection between the behavior and the reward.

One of the many benefits of positive reinforcement is that it strengthens the bond between you and your dog. Rather than fearing punishment, your dog will learn to associate you with positive experiences, leading to a stronger, more trusting relationship. Additionally, positive reinforcement is adaptable to any age or breed of dog, making it a versatile method for training.

It's important to note that positive reinforcement is not about permissiveness. It's not about letting your dog do whatever they want. Rather, it's about teaching them what behaviors are rewarding. Unwanted behaviors are not rewarded, and over time, they will decrease because they do not lead to a positive outcome.

Positive reinforcement is a powerful, effective, and humane method for training dogs. By rewarding desirable behaviors, you can guide your dog towards becoming a well-behaved, happy, and confident companion. Remember, the key to successful positive reinforcement training is consistency, timing, and finding the right motivators for your dog. With patience and persistence, you'll find that positive reinforcement is not only effective but also strengthens the bond between you and your dog.

Common Mistakes to Avoid

While positive reinforcement is a powerful tool for training dogs, it's not foolproof. There are common mistakes that can undermine its effectiveness. By being aware of these pitfalls, you can avoid them and make your training efforts more successful.

One common mistake is inconsistency. Dogs learn best when rules are consistent. If you reward a behavior one day but ignore it the next, your dog will be confused and may not learn the desired behavior. Be consistent with your commands, your expectations, and your rewards.

Another common mistake is timing. The reward must be given immediately after the desired behavior for your dog to make the connection. If the reward comes too late, your dog may not associate it with the behavior you're trying to reinforce.

Over-reliance on treats is another pitfall. While treats are a powerful motivator for most dogs, they should not be the only form of reward. Praise, petting, and play can also be effective rewards. Additionally, if treats are used too frequently, they can lose their effectiveness, and you may find yourself with a dog that will only perform for a treat.

Neglecting to "fade" the reward is another common mistake. Once your dog has learned a new behavior, you should gradually reduce the frequency of treats, replacing them with praise or other non-food rewards. This process, known as "fading," helps ensure that your dog will perform the behavior even when a treat is not forthcoming.

Ignoring "bad" behavior can also be a mistake. While positive reinforcement focuses on rewarding good behavior, it's also important to address unwanted behaviors. However, this doesn't mean punishing your dog. Instead, try to redirect the behavior towards something more positive. For example, if your dog is chewing on a shoe, redirect them to a chew toy, and then reward them for taking the toy.

Failing to make training fun is another common mistake. Training sessions should be enjoyable for both you and your dog. If training feels like a chore, your dog will pick up on your attitude and may become less enthusiastic. Keep sessions short and upbeat, and try to end on a positive note.

Many people make the mistake of thinking that training ends after a behavior is learned. But training is an ongoing process. Even after your dog has mastered a behavior, it's important to continue reinforcing it occasionally to keep it fresh in their mind.

While positive reinforcement is a powerful tool for training dogs, it's important to avoid common mistakes like inconsistency, poor timing, over-reliance on treats, neglecting to fade the reward, ignoring bad behavior, making training a chore, and thinking that training ends. By avoiding these pitfalls, you can make your training efforts more effective and enjoyable for both you and your dog.

Timing and Consistency in Training

Timing and consistency are two of the most critical elements in successful dog training, especially when using positive reinforcement. They can significantly impact the effectiveness of your training sessions and the speed at which your dog learns new behaviors.

Timing refers to when you deliver the reward after your dog performs the desired behavior. For positive reinforcement to work effectively, the reward must be given immediately after the behavior occurs. This is because dogs live in the moment and have a short "learning window." If the reward comes too late, even by a few seconds, your dog may not associate it with the behavior you're trying to reinforce. Instead, they might associate it with whatever they were doing at the moment they received the reward. This can lead to confusion and slower learning.

For example, if you're teaching your dog to sit, the treat or praise should come the instant their bottom touches the ground. If you wait until they've stood back up to give the reward, your dog might think they're being rewarded for standing, not sitting. This immediate reinforcement helps your dog make the connection between the behavior and the reward, reinforcing the behavior you want to see.

Consistency, on the other hand, refers to maintaining the same rules, commands, and rewards across all training sessions and situations. Dogs thrive on consistency. They learn best when the rules are the same every time. If you reward a behavior one day but ignore it the next, or if you use different commands for the same behavior, your dog will become confused, and their learning may stall.

Consistency also applies to everyone in your household. If one person allows the dog on the couch and another person does not, this mixed messaging can confuse your dog and hinder their training progress. Make sure everyone in your home is on the same page about the rules and expectations for your dog.

Timing and consistency are critical to successful dog training. By rewarding your dog immediately after they perform the desired behavior, you can help them make the connection between the behavior and the reward. By being consistent in your commands, expectations, and rewards, you can provide a clear and steady learning environment for your dog. Remember, training is not a one-time event but an ongoing process. With patience, persistence, and the right approach, you can use the power of positive reinforcement to train your dog effectively.

Keeping Training Sessions Engaging

Keeping training sessions engaging is key to maintaining your dog's interest and enthusiasm. Training should be a fun and rewarding experience for both of you, not a chore or a source of frustration. Here are some strategies to keep your training sessions engaging and productive.

Firstly, keep sessions short. Dogs, especially puppies, have short attention spans. Long training sessions can become tedious and your dog may lose focus. Instead, aim for multiple short sessions throughout the day. This keeps training fresh and interesting for your dog, and it can also be more effective, as dogs often learn better in short bursts.

Vary the activities within each session. Repeating the same command over and over can become monotonous for your dog. Mix it up by working on different commands or behaviors in each session. This not only keeps things interesting, but also helps your dog learn to respond to different commands in various contexts.

Use high-value rewards. All rewards are not created equal in the eyes of your dog. Some rewards, like a favorite treat or toy, may hold more value for your dog than others. Use these high-value rewards in training to keep your dog motivated and engaged.

Incorporate play into your training sessions. Play is a powerful motivator for dogs and can make training more fun and engaging. Try incorporating games into your training, or use a favorite toy as a reward. This can make training feel less like work and more like fun.

Be enthusiastic and positive. Your energy and attitude can greatly influence your dog's engagement in training. If you're enthusiastic and positive, your dog is likely to be as well. Use a cheerful voice, give lots of praise, and show excitement when your dog does well. This positive energy can make training more enjoyable for your dog and can boost their motivation to learn.

End each session on a positive note. Always finish with a command your dog knows well, so you can reward them and end with a success. This leaves your dog with a positive impression of training and can make them look forward to the next session.

Keeping training sessions engaging is crucial for effective dog training. By keeping sessions short, varying the activities, using high-value rewards, incorporating play, maintaining a positive attitude, and ending on a positive note, you can keep your dog interested and motivated. Remember, training should be a fun and rewarding experience for both of you. With the right approach, you can make each training session an engaging and productive experience for your dog.

Balancing Treats and Praise

Finding the right balance between treats and praise in dog training can be a delicate task. Both are forms of positive reinforcement and can be highly effective in encouraging desirable behaviors. However, relying too heavily on one or the other can have drawbacks.

Treats are a powerful motivator for most dogs. They provide an immediate, tangible reward that dogs can quickly come to understand and look forward to. However, an over-reliance on treats can lead to a few issues. For one, it can contribute to weight gain if not properly managed. Additionally, if treats are used too frequently, they can lose their effectiveness as a training tool. Your dog may start to expect a treat for every little thing they do, or they may only respond to commands when a treat is visibly present.

On the other hand, praise is a form of reward that can be given freely and frequently without any negative side effects. A kind word, a pat on the head, or a scratch behind the ears can go a long way in making your dog feel loved and appreciated. However, while some dogs are highly motivated by praise, others may not find it as rewarding as a tasty treat.

The key is to find a balance that works for you and your dog. Start by using both treats and praise in your training sessions. As your dog begins to learn a new command, you might use a treat each time they perform the behavior correctly. Pair the treat with verbal praise so that your dog begins to associate the praise with the positive feeling of getting a reward.

As your dog becomes more reliable in performing the behavior, gradually reduce the frequency of treats, but continue to give verbal praise. This process, known as "fading," helps your dog transition from a continuous schedule of reinforcement (getting a treat every time) to an intermittent one (getting a treat some of the time). Over time, your dog should be able to perform the behavior with praise alone serving as the reward.

The goal is not to eliminate treats entirely, but to use them strategically. Treats can still be used occasionally as a special reward, or in situations where you need a high-value motivator, such as training in a distracting environment.

Balancing treats and praise in dog training is all about finding what motivates your dog and using those motivators effectively. By using both treats and praise, and gradually reducing the reliance on treats, you can create a balanced and effective training approach that keeps your dog motivated and eager to learn.

Chapter 6

BASIC OBEDIENCE COMMANDS

Teaching Short Commands (Sit, Stay, Come)

Teaching your dog basic commands like "sit," "stay," and "come" is not only beneficial for their safety but also helps to establish clear communication between you and your pet. These commands are the foundation of obedience training and can be taught using positive reinforcement techniques.

Let's start with "sit." This is often the first command taught because it's simple and useful. To teach "sit," hold a treat close to your dog's nose and then move your hand up, allowing their head to follow the treat and causing their bottom to lower. Once they're in the sitting position, say "sit," give them the treat and share affection. Repeat this sequence a few times every day until your dog has it mastered.

Next is the "stay" command, which is crucial for keeping your dog safe. Before you begin, ensure your dog is proficient at the "sit" command. Ask your dog to "sit," then open the palm of your hand in front of you and say "stay." Take a few steps back. If your dog stays, give them a treat. If they don't, bring them back to the original spot and repeat the process. Start off with short distances, and gradually increase the distance as your dog gets better at staying.

The "come" command is vital in recalling your dog, especially in outdoor environments. To teach this, put a leash and collar on your dog. Go down to their level and say "come" while gently pulling on the leash. When your dog gets to you, reward them with a treat and affection. Once they've mastered it with the leash, try it without.

Remember, when teaching these commands, patience and consistency are key. Keep training sessions short and fun. And always end on a positive note, rewarding your dog for their hard work. It's also important to use the commands in various situations so your dog learns to respond to them no matter what's going on around them.

Teaching your dog the basic commands of "sit," "stay," and "come" is an essential part of their training. These commands not only promote good behavior but also can keep your dog safe in potentially dangerous situations. By using positive reinforcement techniques and practicing patience and consistency, you can successfully teach these commands to your dog, strengthening your bond and enhancing your communication with them.

Essential Commands for Everyday Life

In addition to "sit," "stay," and "come," there are several other commands that are essential for everyday life with your dog. These commands can help ensure your dog's safety, improve their manners, and make your daily routines smoother and more enjoyable.

"Leave it" is a crucial command that can prevent your dog from picking up something dangerous or undesirable. To teach this command, hold a treat in both hands. Show your dog one enclosed fist with the treat inside and say, "leave it." Ignore the behaviors they throw at you to get the treat, and once they stop trying, give them the treat from the other hand. Repeat until your dog moves away from the first fist when you say "leave it." Then, you can gradually progress to more challenging situations.

"Down" is another useful command, especially in situations where you need your dog to be calm and controlled. Start with your dog sitting in front of you. Hold a treat in your hand and lower it slowly to the floor, allowing your dog to follow it with their nose. As their head lowers, their body should naturally move into the down position. Once they're fully down, say "down" and give them the treat.

"Off" is a command that can be used to discourage behaviors like jumping on people or furniture. When your dog jumps up, turn your back to them, ignore the behavior, and say "off." Once all four paws are back on the ground, reward them with praise or a treat. It's important to be consistent with this command and ensure all family members and visitors follow the same protocol.

"Drop it" is a lifesaver in situations where your dog has picked up something they shouldn't have. To teach this, play a game of fetch with a toy. When your dog has the toy in their mouth, hold a treat in front of their nose and say "drop it." Most dogs will drop the toy to get the treat. When they do, give them the treat and praise.

"Heel" is a command that can make walks more enjoyable. It teaches your dog to walk at your side, rather than pulling on the leash. Start by having your dog sit at your left side. With a treat in your left hand, say "heel" and take a few steps forward. If your dog stays at your side, give them the treat and praise. If they pull ahead, stop walking and guide them back to your side.

Commands like "leave it," "down," "off," "drop it," and "heel" are essential for everyday life with your dog. They can help ensure your dog's safety, improve their manners, and make your daily routines smoother. As with all training, teaching these commands requires patience, consistency, and positive reinforcement. With time and practice, your dog can learn to respond reliably to these commands, making life easier and more enjoyable for both of you.

Reinforcing Commands through Repetition

Repetition is a fundamental principle in dog training. Dogs, like humans, learn through repeated experiences. When a behavior is followed by a reward, your dog is likely to repeat that behavior in the hope of earning another reward. This is the basis of positive reinforcement training. However, repetition in dog training is not just about doing the same thing over and over. It's about reinforcing commands in a variety of contexts and gradually increasing the level of difficulty.

When you first start teaching a new command, you'll want to practice it in a quiet, distraction-free environment. This allows your dog to focus on you and the command without being sidetracked by other stimuli. Begin with short training sessions, gradually increasing the length as your dog's attention span improves. Remember to keep the training sessions fun and positive to keep your dog engaged and motivated.

Once your dog is reliably responding to the command in a quiet environment, it's time to start practicing in different locations and adding distractions. This could mean practicing the command in the backyard, at the park, or on a busy street. The goal is to teach your dog to respond to the command no matter where they are or what's going on around them.

Adding distractions gradually is key. You don't want to move from a quiet room to a busy park in one step. Instead, start with minor distractions, like a family member walking by, and gradually increase the level of distraction as your dog becomes more proficient.

Each new environment or level of distraction is a new challenge for your dog. Be patient and be prepared to take a few steps back in your training if necessary. If your dog struggles with a command in a new environment or with a higher level of distraction, go back to a simpler scenario where they can succeed, and gradually build up from there.

Repetition also means practicing the command in various situations throughout the day. For example, you might ask your dog to "sit" before you put their food bowl down, before you put on their leash for a walk, or before you throw a toy for a game of fetch. This not only gives you more opportunities to practice the command, but also helps your dog understand that the command applies in all situations, not just during formal training sessions.

Remember that repetition doesn't mean mindless repetition. Each repetition should be purposeful, with a clear goal in mind. Whether you're working on improving your dog's speed in responding to a command, their ability to perform the command with distractions, or their understanding of the command in different contexts, each repetition should bring you one step closer to that goal.

Reinforcing commands through repetition is a crucial part of dog training. By practicing commands in a variety of contexts, gradually increasing the level of difficulty, and making each repetition purposeful, you can help your dog learn to respond reliably to commands. Remember, patience and consistency are key. With time and practice, your dog can become a well-trained, obedient companion.

Transitioning Commands to Real-Life Scenarios

Transitioning commands to real-life scenarios is a crucial step in your dog's training. It's one thing for your dog to respond to a command in a quiet room during a training session, but it's quite another for them to respond to the same command when they're excited, distracted, or in a new environment. This is where the rubber meets the road in dog training, and it's where you'll see the real benefits of all your hard work.

One of the first steps in transitioning commands to real-life scenarios is to start practicing in a variety of environments. If you've been training in your living room, try moving to the backyard, then to the front yard, then to a quiet street or park. Each new environment presents new distractions, and by practicing in these different settings, you can help your dog learn to focus on you and respond to commands no matter what's going on around them.

Next, start incorporating commands into your daily routines. This not only provides additional opportunities for practice, but also helps your dog understand that commands are not just for training sessions—they're a part of everyday life. For example, you might ask your dog to "sit" before you put their food bowl down, to "stay" while you open the front door, or to "come" when it's time to go inside after a play session in the backyard.

It's also important to practice commands in situations that mimic real-life scenarios your dog is likely to encounter. For example, if you often take your dog to a busy park, practice commands there. If your dog will be spending time in an office or a classroom, practice commands in those types of environments. The more your training mimics real life, the better prepared your dog will be to respond to commands when it really counts.

Transitioning commands to real-life scenarios is likely to be challenging for your dog. Be patient, and be prepared to take a few steps back in your training if necessary. If your dog struggles with a command in a new environment or with a higher level of distraction, go back to a simpler scenario where they can succeed, and gradually build up from there.

Keep in mind that transitioning commands to real-life scenarios is an ongoing process. Even after your dog has mastered a command in a variety of situations, it's important to continue practicing and reinforcing that command regularly. This will help keep the command fresh in your dog's mind and ensure they continue to respond reliably.

Transitioning commands to real-life scenarios is a crucial part of dog training. By practicing in a variety of environments, incorporating commands into daily routines, and mimicking real-life situations, you can help your dog learn to respond to commands reliably when it matters most. Remember, patience and consistency are key. With time and practice, your dog can become a well-trained, obedient companion who is a joy to live with.

Correcting Command Confusion

Command confusion can occur when a dog struggles to understand or differentiate between different commands. This can be frustrating for both the dog and the owner, but with patience, consistency, and the right approach, it can be resolved.

One common cause of command confusion is inconsistency in the use of commands. If different words or signals are used for the same command, or if the same word is used for different commands, your dog can become confused. To avoid this, choose one word or signal for each command and use it consistently. Make sure all family members are on the same page.

If your dog is struggling to differentiate between two commands, go back to basics. Practice each command separately in a distraction-free environment until your dog is responding reliably. Then, start practicing the commands in the same session, but still separately. For example, you might practice "sit" for a few minutes, then take a short break, then practice "down" for a few minutes.

Once your dog is responding reliably to each command when practiced separately, you can start practicing them together. Give the command for "sit," reward your dog for responding, then give the command for "down," and reward your dog for responding. This helps your dog learn to listen for each command and respond appropriately.

If your dog responds to the wrong command, don't reward them. Instead, calmly repeat the correct command. If they continue to struggle, take a step back and practice each command separately again. Remember, patience is key. It can take time for your dog to learn to differentiate between similar commands.

Another common cause of command confusion is advancing too quickly. If you move on to a new command before your dog has fully mastered the previous one, they may get confused. Make sure your dog is responding reliably to a command in a variety of situations before introducing a new command.

Correcting command confusion requires patience, consistency, and a step-by-step approach. By practicing commands separately, using each command consistently, and not advancing too quickly, you can help your dog understand and differentiate between commands. Remember, the goal of training is not just to have a dog who responds to commands, but to build a strong, trusting relationship with your dog. With time and patience, you can achieve both.

Chapter 7

SOCIALIZING YOUR DOG

Importance of Early Socialization

Socialization is a critical aspect of your dog's development, particularly during their early stages of life. It involves introducing your dog to a variety of people, animals, environments, and experiences, which can help them grow into a well-adjusted, confident adult dog. Early socialization can shape your dog's behavior and temperament, and it's considered one of the most crucial elements of responsible dog ownership.

The primary socialization period for dogs is between three and twelve weeks of age. During this time, puppies are most receptive to new experiences. This period is a window of opportunity for owners to expose their dogs to a wide variety of stimuli in a controlled and positive manner. The experiences your dog has during this time can significantly influence their future behavior and reactions.

Early socialization can help prevent behavioral problems later in life. Dogs that are not adequately socialized during this critical period may develop fear, aggression, or anxiety. They may be wary of anything unfamiliar and react negatively or fearfully to new situations. On the other hand, dogs that are well-socialized are typically more confident, adaptable, and less likely to show aggression or fear.

Socialization involves more than just introducing your dog to other dogs. It's about exposing them to a wide range of experiences, including different environments, sounds, smells, people, and animals. This could include walking your dog in various environments, like busy streets, parks, and quiet neighborhoods. It could also involve exposing them to different people, including children, elderly people, and people wearing uniforms or hats. The more varied and positive experiences your dog has, the more likely they are to be comfortable in different situations.

It's essential to ensure that socialization experiences are positive for your dog. Forcing a scared puppy to face their fears can backfire and make their fears worse. Instead, introduce new experiences gradually and use positive reinforcement, like treats and praise, to reward your dog for calm, non-fearful behavior. If your dog seems overwhelmed, take a step back and slow down the process.

While the early socialization period is critical, socialization should be a lifelong process. Continue to expose your dog to varied experiences throughout their life to help them maintain their adaptability and confidence.

Early socialization is a crucial part of your dog's development. It can shape your dog's behavior and temperament, help prevent behavioral problems, and contribute to your dog's overall quality of life. By exposing your dog to a wide range of positive experiences, you can help them grow into a confident, well-adjusted dog. Remember, socialization should be a lifelong process, with new experiences introduced throughout your dog's life.

Socializing with People, Dogs, and New Environments

Socializing your dog with people, other dogs, and new environments is a crucial part of their development. It helps them become well-adjusted, confident, and less likely to exhibit behavioral problems. This process involves gradually introducing your dog to a variety of people, dogs, and environments in a positive and controlled manner.

When socializing your dog with people, it's important to introduce them to a wide range of individuals. This includes people of different ages, sizes, and appearances. Children, elderly people, people wearing hats or uniforms, people with beards, and people carrying umbrellas are all examples of the diversity your dog should be exposed to. Always supervise these interactions to ensure they are positive and safe. Encourage people to approach your dog calmly and to give them space if they seem uncomfortable.

Socializing your dog with other dogs is also essential. Positive interactions with other dogs can help your dog learn important social skills and behaviors. Dog parks, puppy classes, and play dates with other dogs can provide great socialization opportunities. However, it's important to make sure these interactions are positive. Watch for signs of fear or aggression and remove your dog from the situation if they seem uncomfortable.

Introducing your dog to new environments is another key aspect of socialization. This could include urban environments with lots of people and traffic, quiet rural areas, busy parks, and quiet trails. It could also include different types of flooring, stairs, elevators, and car rides. The goal is to help your dog become comfortable in a variety of settings.

When introducing your dog to new people, dogs, or environments, it's important to go at a pace that's comfortable for your dog. If your dog seems scared or overwhelmed, slow down and give them time to adjust. Use positive reinforcement, like treats and praise, to reward your dog for calm, non-fearful behavior.

Socialization is not about overwhelming your dog with new experiences. It's about gradually introducing new experiences in a positive, controlled manner. It's also important to continue socialization throughout your dog's life to help them maintain their confidence and adaptability.

Socializing your dog with people, dogs, and new environments is a crucial part of their development. It can help them become well-adjusted, confident, and less likely to exhibit behavioral problems. By introducing a wide range of positive experiences in a controlled manner, you can help your dog become a well-socialized, happy companion.

Managing Socialization for Older Dogs

While early socialization is crucial, it's never too late to socialize an older dog. Whether you've adopted an adult dog who hasn't been properly socialized, or you've noticed that your own dog has developed some socialization issues, there are strategies you can use to help your dog become more comfortable with new experiences, people, and other animals.

First, it's important to understand that socializing an older dog may take more time and patience than socializing a puppy. Adult dogs can have ingrained behaviors and fears that take time to overcome. But with patience, consistency, and a positive approach, you can help your dog become more confident and well-adjusted.

Just like with puppies, socialization for older dogs involves gradually exposing them to a variety of people, animals, and environments. However, you'll need to be particularly mindful of your dog's comfort level. If your dog shows signs of fear or anxiety, it's important to slow down and not push them too hard. Forcing a scared dog to face their fears can backfire and make their fears worse.

Start with low-stress situations and gradually increase the level of difficulty as your dog becomes more comfortable. For example, you might start by introducing your dog to a calm, friendly person in a quiet environment. Once your dog is comfortable with this, you can gradually introduce more people, more noise, and more activity.

When introducing your dog to new people or animals, it's important to control the situation as much as possible. Ask people to approach your dog calmly and quietly, without making direct eye contact, which can be threatening to dogs. If you're introducing your dog to another dog, choose a neutral location and keep both dogs on leashes at first. Allow them to sniff each other and interact in their own time.

Using positive reinforcement is crucial when socializing an older dog. Reward your dog with treats, praise, or a favorite toy whenever they have a positive interaction with a person, animal, or new environment. This helps your dog associate these experiences with positive outcomes.

Remember that socialization is an ongoing process. Even after your dog seems to be more comfortable with new experiences, continue to expose them to a variety of people, animals, and environments. This will help them maintain their confidence and adaptability.

While socializing an older dog can be challenging, it's certainly possible with patience, consistency, and a positive approach. By gradually introducing new experiences, controlling the situation as much as possible, and using positive reinforcement, you can help your older dog become more comfortable with new experiences, people, and other animals. Remember, the goal of socialization is to help your dog become a confident, well-adjusted member of your family and community.

Introducing New Pets or Babies to Your Dog

Introducing new pets or babies to your dog is an important process that requires careful planning and patience. Whether you're bringing home a new puppy, an adult dog, a cat, or a baby, these changes can be stressful for your existing dog. However, with the right approach, you can help ensure a smooth transition and a positive relationship between your dog and the new addition to your family.

When introducing a new pet, it's important to consider the personalities and energy levels of both animals. A calm, older dog might not appreciate a hyperactive puppy, while a playful dog might be a great match for a lively kitten. It's also important to consider the size and breed of the new pet, as some dogs might not get along with certain breeds or sizes of animals.

The introduction should be done in a controlled, neutral environment. This could be a quiet room in your house, a fenced yard, or a quiet park. Keep both animals on a leash at first, and let them sniff each other and interact in their own time. Watch for signs of aggression or fear, and separate the animals if necessary. Reward both animals with treats and praise for calm, positive interactions.

When introducing a baby to your dog, it's important to start preparing your dog long before the baby arrives. This could involve playing recordings of baby sounds, introducing your dog to the baby's scent (such as a blanket or clothing), and setting up baby equipment like cribs and strollers. This helps your dog get used to the new sights, sounds, and smells associated with the baby.

Once the baby arrives, introduce your dog slowly and calmly. Let your dog sniff the baby's blanket or clothing first, then gradually allow your dog to get closer to the baby over time. Always supervise interactions between your dog and the baby, and never leave them alone together.

In both cases, it's important to maintain your dog's routine as much as possible. Changes in feeding times, walk times, or attention can be stressful for your dog. Try to keep these routines consistent, and make sure your dog is still getting plenty of exercise and attention.

Finally, remember that these introductions take time. Don't rush the process, and be patient with your dog. It might take weeks or even months for your dog to fully adjust to the new addition. But with time, patience, and positive reinforcement, you can help foster a positive relationship between your dog and the new addition to your family.

Introducing new pets or babies to your dog is a significant event that requires careful planning and patience. By preparing your dog in advance, introducing the new addition in a controlled, neutral environment, maintaining your dog's routine, and using positive reinforcement, you can help ensure a smooth transition and a positive relationship between your dog and the new addition. Remember, every dog is unique, and what works for one dog might not work for another. Always consider your dog's personality, needs, and comfort level when introducing new pets or babies.

Avoiding Overstimulation

While socialization is crucial for your dog's development, it's equally important to avoid overstimulation. Overstimulation occurs when your dog is exposed to too many new experiences, sounds, smells, or interactions in a short period. This can lead to stress, anxiety, and even behavioral problems.

One of the key signs of overstimulation is a change in your dog's behavior. They might become hyperactive, start barking or whining excessively, show signs of aggression, or try to hide or escape. Physical signs can include panting, drooling, dilated pupils, or shedding more than usual. If you notice any of these signs, it's important to remove your dog from the situation and give them a chance to calm down.

To avoid overstimulation, it's important to introduce new experiences gradually. Rather than taking your dog to a busy park, a bustling city street, and a crowded pet store all in one day, spread these experiences out over several days or weeks. This gives your dog a chance to process each new experience and recover before moving on to the next one.

It's also important to give your dog plenty of downtime. Just like humans, dogs need time to relax and decompress. Make sure your dog has a quiet, comfortable place where they can rest and recover after a busy day of socialization. This could be a crate, a dog bed, or a quiet room in your house.

Remember that every dog is different. Some dogs are naturally more outgoing and may enjoy a busy day of socialization, while others may prefer quieter, more controlled experiences. Pay attention to your dog's body language and behavior, and adjust your socialization plan to suit their individual needs and comfort level.

While socialization is crucial for your dog's development, it's equally important to avoid overstimulation. By introducing new experiences gradually, giving your dog plenty of downtime, and adjusting your socialization plan to suit your dog's individual needs, you can help ensure that socialization is a positive and beneficial experience for your dog. Remember, the goal of socialization is not to overwhelm your dog with new experiences, but to help them become a confident, well-adjusted member of your family and community.

Chapter 8

PROBLEMATIC BEHAVIOR AND SOLUTIONS

Instinctual vs. Learned Behavior

Understanding the difference between instinctual and learned behavior in dogs is crucial when addressing problematic behaviors. This understanding can help you determine the root cause of a behavior and develop an effective solution.

Instinctual behaviors are innate, meaning they are behaviors that your dog is born with. These behaviors are hard-wired into your dog's brain and are often related to survival. For example, dogs have an instinctual need to chew, which in the wild would help them keep their teeth clean and kill prey. Other instinctual behaviors include digging, chasing, and barking. While these behaviors can be problematic in a domestic setting, it's important to remember that they are natural for dogs.

On the other hand, learned behaviors are those that your dog picks up through their experiences and interactions with their environment. These behaviors can be positive, such as sitting on command, or negative, such as jumping up on people for attention. Learned behaviors can be influenced by a variety of factors, including training, socialization, and reinforcement.

When addressing problematic behaviors, it's important to consider whether the behavior is instinctual or learned. For instinctual behaviors, it can be helpful to provide appropriate outlets for these behaviors. For example, if your dog has a strong instinct to chew, providing them with plenty of chew toys can help satisfy this instinct in a way that doesn't involve your furniture.

For learned behaviors, the solution often involves training and reinforcement. If your dog has learned that jumping up on people gets them attention, for example, you'll need to teach them that this behavior is not rewarded. This could involve ignoring your dog when they jump up and only giving them attention when they have all four paws on the ground.

In both cases, patience and consistency are key. Changing behavior takes time, and it's important to be consistent in your approach. If you sometimes reward a behavior and sometimes punish it, your dog will become confused and the behavior is unlikely to change.

Understanding the difference between instinctual and learned behavior can help you address problematic behaviors in your dog. By providing appropriate outlets for instinctual behaviors and using consistent training and reinforcement for learned behaviors, you can help guide your dog towards more desirable behavior. Remember, patience and consistency are key, and it's important to always consider your dog's natural instincts and needs when addressing problematic behaviors.

Addressing Jumping, Barking, and Begging

Jumping, barking, and begging are common behaviors in dogs that can become problematic if not properly managed. These behaviors are often learned, meaning they are a response to a dog's environment and experiences.

Dogs often jump on people as a way of greeting or seeking attention. While this behavior may seem cute when your dog is a small puppy, it can become a problem as your dog grows larger and stronger. To address this behavior, it's important to teach your dog that jumping does not result in attention. When your dog jumps on you, turn your back and ignore them. Only give them attention when all four paws are on the ground. Consistency is key here - make sure all family members and visitors follow the same rule.

Barking is a natural behavior for dogs and serves as a means of communication. However, excessive barking can become a nuisance. To address this behavior, first try to identify the trigger for the barking. Is your dog barking at a specific stimulus, like a passing car or a squirrel in the yard? If so, try to limit your dog's exposure to this stimulus. If your dog is barking for attention, ignore them until they stop barking, then reward them with attention or a treat. If your dog is barking out of boredom, make sure they are getting enough physical and mental stimulation.

Begging is a behavior that is often inadvertently reinforced by owners. If your dog learns that begging at the table results in tasty scraps of food, they will continue to beg. To address this behavior, it's important to never reward begging with food. Instead, have your dog go to a specific spot, like their bed or crate, during meal times. Reward them for staying in this spot with praise or a treat. If your dog continues to beg, ignore them. Remember, consistency is key. If you sometimes give in to begging, your dog will learn that begging sometimes results in food, which can make the behavior more persistent.

Addressing problematic behaviors like jumping, barking, and begging often involves identifying the cause of the behavior, providing appropriate outlets or alternatives, and using consistent training and reinforcement. Remember, patience is key. Changing behavior takes time, and it's important to be consistent in your approach. By understanding your dog's needs and motivations, you can help guide them towards more desirable behaviors.

Solutions for Chewing, Digging, and Biting

Chewing, digging, and biting are instinctual behaviors for dogs, but they can become problematic if not properly managed. These behaviors can be destructive and potentially dangerous, but with the right approach, they can be effectively addressed.

Chewing is a natural behavior for dogs. It helps them explore their environment, relieves boredom, and can soothe discomfort from teething in puppies or promote oral health in adult dogs. However, inappropriate chewing can lead to destruction of personal belongings or potential ingestion of harmful objects. To manage this behavior, provide your dog with a variety of appropriate chew toys. If your dog chews on something inappropriate, redirect their attention to a suitable chew toy. Using a deterrent spray on furniture or other items can also discourage unwanted chewing.

Digging can be a more challenging behavior to address, as it can be driven by various factors, including boredom, the desire to hide food or find a cool place to lie down, or the instinct to hunt small animals. If your dog is digging out of boredom, providing more physical and mental stimulation can help. This could include more walks, playtime, or puzzle toys. If your dog is digging to hide food, consider feeding them smaller amounts more frequently. If your dog is digging to hunt, try to make your yard less appealing to small animals.

Biting is a behavior that needs to be addressed immediately, as it can lead to serious consequences. Puppies often bite during play or when teething, but it's important to teach them bite inhibition from a young age. This can be done by letting out a high-pitched yelp when your puppy bites too hard, then ending playtime. This teaches your puppy that biting too hard leads to an end to fun. For adult dogs, biting can be a sign of fear or aggression and may require help from a professional dog trainer or behaviorist.

In all cases, punishment is not an effective solution and can often exacerbate the problem. Instead, focus on redirecting the behavior, providing appropriate outlets, and rewarding good behavior. And remember, patience and consistency are key. Changing behavior takes time, and it's important to be consistent in your approach.

Chewing, digging, and biting are instinctual behaviors that can become problematic if not properly managed. By understanding the root cause of these behaviors and providing appropriate outlets and redirection, you can help guide your dog towards more desirable behaviors. Remember, patience and consistency are key, and punishment is not an effective solution. By approaching these behaviors with understanding and patience, you can help your dog become a well-behaved member of your family.

Setting Boundaries and Routines

Creating a structured environment with clear boundaries and routines is one of the most effective ways to manage problematic behaviors in dogs. Dogs are creatures of habit, and they thrive when they know what to expect. Setting boundaries and routines can provide your dog with a sense of security and help prevent behavioral issues.

Setting boundaries involves defining what behaviors are acceptable and where. This might include rules like not allowing your dog on the furniture, not begging at the table, or staying out of certain rooms. It's important to be consistent with these boundaries. If you allow your dog to break the rules occasionally, they will learn that the rules are negotiable, which can lead to confusion and inconsistent behavior.

To enforce these boundaries, use positive reinforcement. When your dog respects a boundary, reward them with praise, a treat, or a favorite toy. If your dog breaks a boundary, redirect them in a calm, firm manner. Avoid yelling or physical punishment, as this can lead to fear and anxiety, which can exacerbate behavioral issues.

Establishing routines can also be beneficial. Dogs are creatures of habit, and they find comfort in predictability. Routines can help reduce anxiety and prevent problematic behaviors. Your routine might include regular feeding times, walks, playtime, and bedtime. Try to keep these activities consistent from day to day.

Routines can also be used to manage specific behaviors. For example, if your dog begs at the table, establish a routine where your dog goes to their bed or crate during meal times. If your dog jumps on guests, establish a routine where your dog goes to a specific spot when guests arrive. Over time, your dog will learn to associate these events with their routine, which can help prevent problematic behaviors.

Remember, setting boundaries and routines takes time and patience. It's important to be consistent and to reinforce the boundaries and routines regularly. It's also important to make sure all family members are on board and follow the same rules. If one person allows the dog on the couch while another does not, it can confuse the dog and make it harder for them to understand the boundaries.

Setting boundaries and routines can be an effective way to manage problematic behaviors in dogs. By being consistent, using positive reinforcement, and having patience, you can create a structured environment that helps your dog understand what is expected of them. This can lead to a happier, more well-behaved dog, and a more harmonious household. Remember, every dog is unique, and what works for one dog may not work for another. Always consider your dog's individual needs and personality when setting boundaries and routines.

Correcting Behavior with Positive Techniques

Correcting behavior with positive techniques is a cornerstone of modern dog training. This approach focuses on rewarding good behavior, rather than punishing bad behavior. The theory behind this is simple: behaviors that are rewarded are more likely to be repeated, while behaviors that are not rewarded will eventually fade away.

Positive reinforcement can take many forms. It could be a tasty treat, a favorite toy, praise, or a belly rub. The key is to find what motivates your dog and use that as a reward. When your dog behaves in a way that you want, reward them immediately. This helps your dog make the connection between the behavior and the reward.

For example, if your dog has a habit of jumping up on guests, try this positive technique: ask your dog to sit when guests arrive. If your dog sits, give them a treat or a pat on the head. If your dog jumps up, ignore them. Don't scold or push them away, as this can be seen as attention. Instead, wait for your dog to calm down, then ask them to sit again. When they do, reward them. Over time, your dog will learn that sitting gets them a reward, while jumping up gets them nothing.

It's also important to set your dog up for success. This means managing their environment to reduce the chances of unwanted behavior. For example, if your dog likes to chew shoes, make sure shoes are put away and provide plenty of appropriate chew toys.

Patience and consistency are key. Changing behavior takes time, and it's important to reward your dog consistently for good behavior. And always end training sessions on a positive note, with a behavior your dog does well. This leaves your dog with a positive impression of training, which can make them more eager to participate in the future.

Correcting behavior with positive techniques is a powerful tool in dog training. By rewarding good behavior, managing your dog's environment, and being patient and consistent, you can help guide your dog towards more desirable behaviors. Remember, the goal is not to punish your dog for bad behavior, but to teach them what behavior is rewarded. This approach not only helps correct problematic behavior, but also strengthens the bond between you and your dog.

Chapter 9

ADVANCED OBEDIENCE AND FUN COMMANDS

Advanced Commands: Heel, Stay, Leave It

After mastering basic commands like "sit", "down", and "come", you may want to introduce your dog to more advanced commands. These commands not only provide mental stimulation for your dog but also enhance your control and communication. Three such commands are "heel", "stay", and "leave it".

"Heel" is a command that instructs your dog to walk closely by your side. This can be particularly useful in crowded or distracting environments. To teach "heel", start by having your dog sit at your side. Begin walking and use a treat to lure your dog into the correct position at your side. As your dog follows the treat, use the command "heel". When your dog is walking nicely at your side, reward them with the treat and praise. Remember, consistency is key. Always have your dog heel on the same side and reward them for staying close to you.

"Stay" is a command that instructs your dog to remain in their current position until given a release command. This command is essential for safety and control. Start by asking your dog to sit or lie down. Then, with a treat in your hand, say "stay" and take a step back. If your dog remains in position, return to them, say "yes" or "good", and give them the treat. Gradually increase the distance and duration of the stay. If your dog breaks the stay, calmly say "oops" and return them to the original position to start again.

"Leave it" is a command that instructs your dog to ignore or drop something. This can be a lifesaver if your dog picks up something dangerous or undesirable. To teach "leave it", hold a treat in your closed hand and present it to your dog. When your dog tries to get the treat, say "leave it". Once your dog stops trying to get the treat and pulls away, say "yes" or "good", and reward them with a different treat. The goal is for your dog to learn that leaving something alone leads to a better reward.

Advanced commands like "heel", "stay", and "leave it" can significantly enhance your control and communication with your dog. They require patience, consistency, and plenty of positive reinforcement to master. Remember, training should be a fun and rewarding experience for both you and your dog. Always end training sessions on a positive note, and don't be afraid to go back to basics if your dog is struggling with a new command. With time and practice, your dog will become a master of advanced obedience.

Building Focus and Impulse Control

Building focus and impulse control in your dog is a critical part of advanced obedience training. These skills are not only beneficial for training purposes but also for your dog's overall behavior and safety.

Focus refers to your dog's ability to pay attention to you, even in the presence of distractions. A dog with good focus will be more responsive to commands and easier to train. To build focus, start by training in a quiet, distraction-free environment. Use high-value treats and make training sessions fun and engaging. Gradually introduce distractions, starting with mild ones and slowly working up to more challenging ones. Reward your dog for maintaining focus on you in the presence of these distractions.

Impulse control is your dog's ability to resist immediate temptations and wait for a better reward. This is an essential skill for preventing problematic behaviors such as jumping, barking, and pulling on the leash. Teaching impulse control often involves exercises that require your dog to wait or hold back in return for a reward.

One effective exercise for building impulse control is the "leave it" command, as discussed earlier. Another exercise is the "stay" command, which requires your dog to remain in one place until given a release command. You can also practice impulse control during feeding times by asking your dog to sit and wait patiently while you prepare their food.

A game that can help build both focus and impulse control is the "name game". Say your dog's name in a cheerful tone. When they look at you, reward them with a treat or praise. Repeat this exercise several times a day, gradually increasing the level of distraction. This game teaches your dog to focus on you when they hear their name, even in a distracting environment.

Building focus and impulse control takes time and patience. Start with short training sessions and gradually increase the duration as your dog's skills improve. Always end training sessions on a positive note to keep your dog motivated and eager to learn.

Building focus and impulse control is an essential part of advanced obedience training. These skills can significantly enhance your dog's responsiveness to commands and prevent problematic behaviors. With patience, consistency, and positive reinforcement, you can help your dog develop strong focus and impulse control. Remember, the goal of training is not just to have a well-behaved dog, but also to strengthen your bond with your dog and make life more enjoyable for both of you.

Teaching Tricks: Roll Over, Spin, High Five

Teaching your dog tricks can be a fun and rewarding experience for both of you. Not only do tricks provide mental stimulation for your dog, but they also offer a great opportunity for bonding. Three fun and relatively simple tricks to start with are "roll over", "spin", and "high five".

"Roll over" is a classic dog trick that can be taught in a few simple steps. Start with your dog in a 'down' position. Hold a treat close to their nose, then move the treat from their nose towards their shoulder, luring them to roll onto their side. Continue moving the treat so that your dog follows it with their nose, rolling over onto their back and then onto their other side. As your dog completes the roll, say "roll over" and give them the treat. Repeat this process, gradually saying "roll over" earlier until your dog begins to associate the command with the action.

"Spin" is a fun trick that can be taught in a similar way. With your dog standing, hold a treat close to their nose and slowly move the treat in a circle around your dog's head, luring them to spin in a circle. As your dog completes the spin, say "spin" and give them the treat. Repeat this process, gradually saying "spin" earlier until your dog begins to associate the command with the action.

"High five" is a trick that can impress your friends and family. Start with your dog in a 'sit' position. Hold a treat in one hand and present your other hand to your dog at about chest height. Most dogs will naturally paw at your hand. When your dog touches your hand with their paw, say "high five" and give them the treat. If your dog doesn't naturally paw at your hand, you can gently tap their paw with your hand to prompt them. Repeat this process until your dog begins to associate the command "high five" with the action.

When teaching tricks, patience and positive reinforcement are key. If your dog is struggling with a trick, take a break and try again later. Always end training sessions on a positive note to keep your dog motivated and eager to learn. And most importantly, have fun! Training should be a fun and rewarding experience for both you and your dog.

Teaching your dog tricks like "roll over", "spin", and "high five" can be a fun and rewarding experience. These tricks provide mental stimulation for your dog and offer a great opportunity for bonding.

With patience, consistency, and positive reinforcement, you can teach your dog these and many other tricks. Remember, the goal of training is not just to have a well-behaved dog, but also to strengthen your bond with your dog and make life more enjoyable for both of you.

Exercise and Enrichment Activities

Exercise and enrichment activities are vital for a dog's physical health and mental well-being. They not only help to keep your dog fit and healthy but also stimulate their mind, reduce boredom, and help to prevent behavioral issues.

Exercise needs can vary greatly depending on your dog's breed, age, and health. Generally, dogs should get at least one hour of exercise each day, but some active breeds may require more. The type of exercise also matters. A walk around the block is a good start, but engaging your dog's mind and allowing them to use their natural instincts is even better.

Activities like fetch, tug-of-war, or hide and seek can be fun and physically demanding for your dog. These games also provide an opportunity for you to interact and bond with your dog. Remember, safety first. Always use toys appropriate for your dog's size and chew strength, and monitor your dog during play to prevent any accidents.

Enrichment activities are designed to challenge your dog's mind and engage their senses. These activities often involve problem-solving, exploration, and learning. Food puzzle toys, for example, not only provide a mental challenge but also slow down eating, which can be beneficial for dogs that eat too quickly. Scent games, where you hide treats or toys and encourage your dog to find them, can engage your dog's powerful sense of smell and natural desire to hunt.

Training sessions are another great form of mental stimulation. Whether you're teaching basic obedience, advanced tricks, or agility, training challenges your dog's mind and strengthens the bond between you. Remember to keep training sessions short and fun. Aim for a few minutes of training at a time, and always end on a positive note.

Socialization is also a form of enrichment. This involves exposing your dog to a variety of people, environments, and other animals in a positive way. This can help to build confidence, reduce fear and anxiety, and promote good behavior.

Remember, every dog is unique. It's important to find what types of exercise and enrichment activities your dog enjoys and benefits from the most. Always consider your dog's individual needs, and be sure to consult with a vet if you have any concerns about your dog's exercise or enrichment routine.

Exercise and enrichment activities play a crucial role in your dog's physical health and mental well-being. By providing a variety of physical exercises and mentally stimulating activities, you can help to keep your dog fit, mentally sharp, and happy. Remember, a tired dog is a good dog, and a mentally stimulated dog is a happy dog.

Tailoring Commands for Challenging Environments

Tailoring commands for challenging environments is an essential part of advanced obedience training. Dogs, like humans, can behave differently in various settings. They might be perfectly obedient at home but become distracted or anxious in a new environment. This is why it's important to practice commands in different settings and gradually introduce distractions to ensure your dog can respond reliably no matter the situation.

Begin by mastering commands in a quiet, familiar environment like your home. Once your dog is responding consistently, gradually introduce distractions. This could be as simple as practicing commands while the TV is on or while other family members are present. The goal is to gradually increase the level of distraction while ensuring your dog can still respond to commands.

Next, practice commands in different environments. Start with quiet, controlled settings like your backyard or a quiet park. Gradually move to more challenging environments like a busy park, a pet store, or a sidewalk near traffic. Always ensure your dog is safe and secure in these environments, and be aware of potential hazards like other dogs, traffic, or distractions that could cause your dog to run off.

It's important to set your dog up for success. Don't move to a more challenging environment or introduce a higher level of distraction until your dog is consistently responding to commands at the current level. If your dog struggles in a new environment, take a step back and practice in a less challenging setting before trying again.

Patience and positive reinforcement are key. Always reward your dog for responding to commands, especially in challenging environments or in the presence of distractions. This will help your dog associate obeying commands with positive outcomes, regardless of the environment or distractions present.

Tailoring commands for challenging environments is a crucial part of advanced obedience training. By gradually introducing distractions and practicing in different settings, you can ensure your dog responds reliably to commands in any situation. Remember, training is a journey, not a destination. It's about building a strong, trusting relationship with your dog, improving communication, and ensuring your dog's safety and well-being. With patience, consistency, and positive reinforcement, you and your dog can enjoy the journey together.

Chapter 10

HEALTH, HYGIENE, AND FIRST AID

Basics of Dog Grooming and Hygiene

Maintaining your dog's grooming and hygiene is an essential part of pet care. Regular grooming not only keeps your dog looking their best but also promotes their overall health and well-being.

One of the most basic grooming tasks is regular brushing. Brushing your dog's coat helps to remove loose hair, distribute natural oils, and keep the coat clean and shiny. The frequency and type of brushing required can vary depending on your dog's breed and coat type. Short-haired breeds may only need weekly brushing, while long-haired breeds may require daily grooming to prevent matting and tangling. Always use a brush suitable for your dog's coat type.

Bathing is another important aspect of dog grooming. How often you should bathe your dog can depend on their breed, coat type, and lifestyle. Some dogs may need a bath every few weeks, while others may only need a bath every few months. Always use a dog-specific shampoo, as human shampoo can be too harsh for a dog's skin. Be sure to rinse thoroughly to remove all shampoo, as leftover residue can cause skin irritation.

Ear care is also important. Check your dog's ears regularly for signs of infection, such as redness, swelling, or a bad smell. Some breeds, especially those with floppy ears, are more prone to ear infections and may require regular cleaning. Always use a vet-recommended ear cleaner and avoid inserting anything into your dog's ear canal, as this can cause injury.

Eye care is another aspect of grooming that shouldn't be overlooked. Regularly check your dog's eyes for signs of irritation or infection, such as redness, discharge, or excessive tearing. Some breeds are prone to tear staining and may require regular cleaning. Always use a vet-recommended eye cleaner and be gentle to avoid causing injury.

Regular grooming sessions also provide an opportunity to check your dog's skin for any abnormalities, such as lumps, bumps, or parasites like fleas and ticks. If you notice anything unusual, it's always a good idea to consult with a vet.

Regular grooming and hygiene are essential for maintaining your dog's health and well-being. By brushing regularly, bathing as needed, and taking care of your dog's ears and eyes, you can help to keep your dog looking and feeling their best. Remember, grooming is also a great opportunity to bond with your dog and check for any signs of health issues. With patience, consistency, and the right tools, grooming can be a rewarding experience for both you and your dog.

Dental Health and Nail Care

Dental health and nail care are two often overlooked aspects of dog care, yet they are vital for your pet's overall health and comfort. Regular attention to these areas can prevent problems down the line and keep your dog in top shape.

Dental health in dogs is as important as it is in humans. Poor dental hygiene can lead to a variety of problems, including bad breath, gum disease, and even systemic infections affecting the heart, liver, and kidneys. Regular brushing is the best way to maintain your dog's dental health. Aim to brush your dog's teeth daily, or at least several times a week. Use a toothbrush and toothpaste designed specifically for dogs. Human toothpaste can be harmful to dogs if swallowed.

Start slowly when introducing tooth brushing to your dog. Let them taste the toothpaste and get used to the feeling of the brush on their teeth and gums. Gradually increase the amount of brushing as your dog becomes more comfortable. If your dog absolutely refuses to allow tooth brushing, consider dental chews, toys, and a diet formulated to promote dental health as alternatives. However, these should not replace brushing but rather supplement it.

Regular vet check-ups should also include dental exams. Sometimes, professional cleanings under anesthesia may be necessary to remove tartar and assess dental health more thoroughly.

Nail care is another critical aspect of your dog's overall health. Overgrown nails can be painful for your dog and can lead to problems walking or running. Depending on your dog's activity level and the surfaces they walk on, you may need to trim their nails anywhere from once a week to once a month.

Use a dog nail trimmer and be careful to avoid cutting into the quick, the sensitive part of the nail that contains blood vessels and nerves. If your dog's nails are dark, this can be difficult to see, so only trim a little bit of the nail at a time. If you're uncomfortable trimming your dog's nails yourself, a vet or groomer can do it for you.

Just like with grooming, introducing dental care and nail trimming should be a gradual process. Use plenty of positive reinforcement to make these experiences as stress-free as possible for your dog. Patience, gentleness, and consistency are key.

Maintaining your dog's dental health and taking care of their nails are essential aspects of their overall health and well-being. Regular tooth brushing, dental check-ups, and nail trims can prevent health issues and keep your dog comfortable. As with all aspects of dog care, these tasks are also opportunities to strengthen your bond with your dog. With patience and consistency, they can become a regular part of your dog's routine.

Handling Common Health Emergencies

Handling common health emergencies in dogs is a skill that every dog owner should have. While it's crucial to seek veterinary care in these situations, knowing what to do in the moment can make a significant difference in your dog's outcome.

One common emergency is choking. If your dog is choking, they may paw at their mouth, have difficulty breathing, or make choking sounds. If your dog is conscious, you can try to remove the object causing the choking by opening your dog's mouth and using a pair of pliers or tweezers. If you can't remove the object or your dog becomes unconscious, you may need to perform a modified version of the Heimlich maneuver by giving sharp blows to your dog's chest.

Another common emergency is heatstroke. Dogs can overheat quickly in hot weather, especially if they are left in a car or don't have access to shade or water. Signs of heatstroke include excessive panting, drooling, red or pale gums, and lethargy. If you suspect your dog has heatstroke, move them to a cool area, offer small amounts of water, and wet their coat with cool (not cold) water. Seek veterinary care immediately.

Poisoning is another emergency that requires immediate attention. Common toxins for dogs include certain foods (like chocolate, grapes, and onions), medications, and antifreeze. Signs of poisoning can vary but may include vomiting, diarrhea, drooling, seizures, and loss of consciousness. If you suspect your dog has ingested a toxin, contact your vet or a pet poison control center right away. If possible, provide them with information about what your dog ingested and how much.

In any emergency, it's crucial to stay calm and act quickly. Contact your vet or an emergency vet clinic as soon as possible. They can provide guidance and prepare for your arrival if immediate veterinary care is needed.

Remember, prevention is the best medicine. Keep potential toxins out of your dog's reach, never leave your dog in a hot car, provide plenty of shade and water on hot days, and always supervise your dog while they are eating or playing with toys.

Knowing how to handle common health emergencies can be lifesaving for your dog. While immediate veterinary care is crucial, your actions in the moment can make a significant difference. Stay calm, act quickly, and always err on the side of caution by seeking veterinary care if you're unsure. Your dog depends on you for their health and safety, and being prepared for emergencies is a key part of responsible dog ownership.

Recognizing When to See the Vet

Recognizing when to seek veterinary care is a critical aspect of responsible pet ownership. While some signs of illness in dogs are obvious, others can be subtle and easy to miss. Being able to identify these signs can help you get your dog the care they need as quickly as possible.

One of the most obvious signs that your dog needs to see a vet is a change in eating or drinking habits. If your dog suddenly loses their appetite or starts drinking more or less water than usual, it's a good idea to consult with a vet. These changes can be signs of various health issues, including dental problems, kidney disease, or even cancer.

Changes in behavior can also be a sign that something is wrong. If your dog is usually active and playful but suddenly becomes lethargic and uninterested in their favorite activities, they may be feeling unwell. On the other hand, a usually calm dog that becomes restless or agitated may also be in discomfort or pain.

Changes in your dog's bathroom habits are another sign that they may need to see a vet. Frequent urination, difficulty urinating, or changes in the color or consistency of your dog's stool can all be signs of health problems.

Unexplained weight loss or gain can also be a sign of illness. While changes in weight can be related to diet and exercise, sudden or dramatic changes can indicate a health issue.

Visible signs of illness, such as vomiting, diarrhea, coughing, or difficulty breathing, should always be addressed by a vet. Other visible signs to look out for include a dull coat, red or swollen gums, a swollen belly, or a limp.

It's important to remember that dogs are good at hiding pain and discomfort, a trait inherited from their wild ancestors who needed to hide signs of weakness from predators. Therefore, any change in your dog's behavior, no matter how subtle, is worth noting.

Regular check-ups are also important, even if your dog seems perfectly healthy. Many health issues can be detected during a routine vet visit before they become serious. Regular check-ups also give you the opportunity to ask your vet any questions you have about your dog's health or behavior.

Being able to recognize when your dog needs to see a vet is a crucial part of keeping them healthy. Any changes in behavior, eating or drinking habits, bathroom habits, or appearance should be taken seriously. Regular vet check-ups are also important for early detection of health issues. Remember, when it comes to your dog's health, it's always better to be safe than sorry. Your dog depends on you for their health and well-being, and being vigilant about their health is one of the best ways you can show your love for them.

Basic Dog First Aid Kit

A basic dog first aid kit is an essential tool for every dog owner. In the event of an emergency, having the right supplies on hand can make a significant difference. While it's important to seek veterinary care in serious situations, a first aid kit can provide temporary relief and stabilization.

Your dog's first aid kit should include bandages and gauze pads to cover wounds and control bleeding. These should be non-stick and safe for use on dogs. Medical tape is also necessary to secure bandages.

Antiseptic wipes or solution can be used to clean wounds before bandaging. It's important to have a gentle, pet-safe option to avoid causing further discomfort or irritation.

A digital thermometer can help you check your dog's temperature. Remember, the normal body temperature for dogs is higher than humans, typically around 101.5 degrees Fahrenheit.

Tweezers can be useful for removing splinters or ticks. If you live in an area where ticks are common, a tick removal tool might also be a good addition to your kit.

A blanket can provide warmth and comfort in stressful situations. It can also be used to carry an injured dog if necessary.

Hydrogen peroxide can induce vomiting in dogs if they ingest something toxic, but it should only be used under the direction of a vet or poison control center.

An emergency contact list is another important item to include in your first aid kit. This should include the numbers for your regular vet, an emergency vet clinic, and a pet poison control center.

Finally, remember to check your first aid kit regularly and replace any items that have been used or expired.

A basic dog first aid kit is a valuable tool in emergency situations. While it's not a substitute for veterinary care, it can provide temporary relief and stabilization. Having a well-stocked first aid kit and knowing how to use the items in it can give you peace of mind and help you better care for your dog in an emergency.

Chapter 11

OUTDOOR ADVENTURES AND SAFETY

Hiking and Camping with Your Dog

Hiking and camping with your dog can be a rewarding experience for both of you. It provides a great opportunity for exercise, exploration, and bonding. However, it's crucial to ensure your dog's safety and enjoyment during these outdoor adventures.

Before setting out on a hike or camping trip, check the regulations of the area. Not all trails or campsites allow dogs, and those that do often have specific rules regarding leashes and waste disposal. Always keep your dog on a leash to protect them from wildlife, prevent them from disturbing other people or animals, and keep them safe from potential hazards.

Ensure your dog is in good health and physically capable of the activity. Hiking can be strenuous, and not all dogs are suited for long or challenging hikes. Consider your dog's age, fitness level, and breed. Brachycephalic breeds, for example, can struggle with strenuous exercise due to their short noses.

Prepare for the hike by packing enough water for both you and your dog, along with a collapsible water bowl for your dog to drink from. Bring dog-friendly snacks for energy, and don't forget poop bags for waste disposal.

Protect your dog from pests and the elements. Use a vet-approved tick and flea preventative, and check your dog for ticks after the hike. In hot weather, avoid hiking during the warmest part of the day and watch for signs of overheating. In cold weather, your dog may need a jacket or booties for protection.

When camping with your dog, keep them in the tent with you at night. This will protect them from the elements and wildlife. Never leave your dog alone at the campsite.

Train your dog to behave well during the hike or camp. They should be able to respond to basic commands like "sit," "stay," and "come." This can help you manage their behavior and keep them safe.

Hiking and camping with your dog can be a fun and rewarding experience. However, it's important to prepare adequately, consider your dog's capabilities, and take steps to ensure their safety. With the right preparation and precautions, you and your dog can enjoy many outdoor adventures together.

Water Safety: Swimming and Boating

Water activities like swimming and boating can be a great way to cool off and have fun with your dog during the warmer months.

However, it's important to keep safety in mind anytime your dog is near water.

Not all dogs are natural swimmers, and even those who are can get into trouble in water that's too deep or has strong currents. Never force your dog into the water. Instead, let them explore at their own pace. If your dog enjoys swimming, consider investing in a dog life jacket, especially if you'll be swimming in deep water. A life jacket can provide extra buoyancy and make it easier for your dog to stay afloat.

When boating with your dog, a life jacket is a must. Choose a life jacket that fits your dog well and has a handle on the back, which you can use to lift your dog out of the water if necessary. Make sure your dog has a shady spot to rest on the boat and plenty of fresh water to drink.

Whether you're swimming or boating, always keep a close eye on your dog. Never leave them unattended near water. Be aware of potential hazards, such as strong currents, waves, and underwater debris. After swimming, rinse your dog off with fresh water to remove chlorine, salt, or algae that could irritate their skin.

It's also important to be mindful of water temperature. Water that's too cold can cause hypothermia, while water that's too warm can lead to overheating. As a rule of thumb, if the water is too cold or hot for you, it's likely too cold or hot for your dog as well.

Remember to respect the local wildlife and ecosystem. Keep your dog from chasing wildlife and follow all rules and regulations regarding dogs and water activities in your area.

Water activities can be a lot of fun for you and your dog, but safety should always be the top priority. With the right precautions, you and your dog can enjoy swimming and boating safely. Always supervise your dog near water, invest in a good-quality life jacket, and be aware of the conditions. With these measures in place, you're all set for a fun and safe day on the water.

Preparing for Long Walks and Runs

Long walks and runs can be an excellent way for both you and your dog to get exercise and enjoy the outdoors. However, just as you would prepare yourself for these activities, it's important to prepare your dog as well.

Before embarking on long walks or runs, make sure your dog is physically capable and in good health. Puppies, older dogs, or dogs with health issues may not be suited for long distances or strenuous activity. Always consult with your vet before starting a new exercise regimen with your dog.

Start slowly and gradually increase the distance and pace of your walks or runs. This gives your dog time to build up their endurance and strength. Pay attention to your dog's signals. If they seem tired, slow down or take a break. Pushing your dog too hard can lead to injuries or health issues.

Hydration is crucial during long walks or runs. Always bring plenty of water for both you and your dog. Consider carrying a collapsible water bowl for your dog to drink from. Remember, dogs can't sweat like humans do, so they can overheat more easily. Avoid exercising during the hottest part of the day and watch for signs of overheating, such as excessive panting, drooling, or lethargy.

Proper nutrition is also important. Your dog may need more food to fuel their increased activity level. However, avoid feeding your dog immediately before or after exercise to prevent stomach upset or a serious condition called bloat.

Don't forget about paw care. Long distances on rough or hot surfaces can be tough on your dog's paws. Check their paws regularly for signs of injury, such as cuts, blisters, or burns. In hot weather, test the pavement with your hand before setting out. If it's too hot for your hand, it's too hot for your dog's paws.

Finally, always keep your dog on a leash for their safety and the safety of others. Even well-trained dogs can get distracted or startled. A leash gives you control and ensures your dog stays with you.

Preparing for long walks or runs with your dog involves more than just lacing up your sneakers and heading out the door. By considering your dog's physical capabilities, starting slowly, staying hydrated, providing proper nutrition, caring for their paws, and using a leash, you can ensure that these activities are safe and enjoyable for your dog. With the right preparation, long walks and runs can be a great way for you and your dog to stay fit and enjoy your time together.

Safety Tips for Different Seasons

As the seasons change, so do the considerations for your dog's safety and comfort during outdoor adventures. Each season brings its own set of challenges and opportunities, and being aware of these can help ensure your dog stays healthy and happy all year round.

In the spring, the warming weather and blooming plants can be a delight for you and your dog. However, this season also sees an increase in allergens and pests. Monitor your dog for signs of allergies, such as itching, redness, or sneezing, and consult your vet if you notice any symptoms. Spring is also when ticks and fleas become more active, so make sure your dog is up-to-date on their parasite prevention.

Summer can be a great time for swimming and other water activities, but the heat can pose a risk. Never leave your dog in a parked car, as the temperature inside can quickly rise to dangerous levels. Provide plenty of shade and fresh water during outdoor activities, and avoid strenuous exercise during the hottest part of the day. Be mindful of hot pavement, which can burn your dog's paws.

Autumn brings cooler weather, which can be a relief after the heat of summer. However, this season also brings certain hazards, such as mushrooms and other fungi that can be toxic if ingested. Keep your dog on a leash and away from areas where these might grow. Fall is also the start of hunting season in many areas, so be aware of local hunting activities and consider using a bright-colored vest or collar for your dog for visibility.

Winter can be a magical time for dogs, with many enjoying playtime in the snow. However, the cold weather can also pose risks. Limit outdoor time in extreme cold, and consider a dog coat or sweater, especially for small, short-haired, or older dogs. Wipe your dog's paws after walks to remove any ice, snow, or salt, which can be irritating or harmful if ingested. Be aware of the risk of hypothermia and frostbite and seek immediate veterinary care if you notice signs, such as shivering, lethargy, or skin discoloration.

In all seasons, remember that changes in weather and daylight hours can affect your dog's behavior and energy levels. Be flexible and willing to adapt your routine to keep your dog comfortable and engaged.

Each season brings its own joys and challenges for outdoor activities with your dog. By being aware of the potential hazards and taking appropriate precautions, you can ensure that your dog stays safe and enjoys the outdoors all year round. Whether it's spring blooms, summer swims, autumn hikes, or winter snow play, every season can be a season of fun and adventure for you and your dog.

Avoiding Common Outdoor Hazards

Outdoor adventures with your dog can be a wonderful way to explore and enjoy nature together. However, the great outdoors also presents a variety of potential hazards for your canine companion. Being aware of these and knowing how to avoid them can help ensure that your outdoor activities are safe and enjoyable for both of you.

One common outdoor hazard is wildlife. Depending on where you live or are adventuring, you might encounter anything from snakes to bears. Always keep your dog on a leash and be aware of your surroundings. Teach your dog to leave wildlife alone, both for their safety and the welfare of the animals.

Plants can also pose a risk. Some plants are toxic to dogs if ingested, and others can cause skin irritation. Familiarize yourself with the common hazardous plants in your area and keep your dog away from them.

Pests like ticks and fleas can be more than just a nuisance. They can transmit diseases that can be serious or even fatal. Use a vet-approved tick and flea preventative, and check your dog for ticks after spending time outdoors.

Heat and cold can both be dangerous if not properly managed. In hot weather, avoid strenuous activity during the warmest part of the day and provide plenty of water and shade. In cold weather, limit time spent outside and consider using a dog coat or sweater for extra warmth.

Water can be a hazard if your dog isn't a strong swimmer or if the water is rough or fast-moving. Always supervise your dog around water and consider using a dog life jacket for added safety.

Lastly, human litter can be a hazard if ingested or stepped on. Keep your dog away from any litter you come across and consider carrying a bag to pick up and dispose of litter safely.

While the outdoors can present certain hazards, being aware of these and taking appropriate precautions can help keep your dog safe. Remember, the goal is to enjoy the outdoors together, and that means making sure your adventures are as safe as they are fun. With a little preparation and vigilance, you and your dog can enjoy countless outdoor adventures together.

Chapter 12

DIET AND NUTRITION FOR EVERY STAGE

Choosing the Right Food for Your Dog's Age

Choosing the right food for your dog is crucial for their health and well-being. Just as human dietary needs change with age, so do those of our canine companions. Understanding these changes can help you provide the best nutrition for your dog at every stage of their life.

Puppies have different nutritional needs than adult dogs. They require more protein to support their rapid growth and development, as well as higher levels of certain nutrients, such as calcium. Puppy food is specially formulated to meet these needs. It's typically recommended to feed puppies a diet specifically designed for them until they reach about 80% of their expected adult size, which can be anywhere from 9 months to 2 years depending on the breed.

Once your dog reaches adulthood, their nutritional needs will change again. Adult dogs require a balanced diet that includes protein, carbohydrates, fats, vitamins, and minerals. However, they need less protein and calcium than puppies. Feeding an adult dog a diet that's too high in protein or calcium can lead to health problems.

The size and breed of your dog can also influence their dietary needs. For example, small breed dogs often require more calories per pound than larger breeds because they have faster metabolisms. Certain breeds may also be prone to specific health issues that can be managed with diet.

As your dog enters their senior years, their dietary needs will change yet again. Older dogs are often less active than their younger counterparts and may require fewer calories to prevent weight gain. However, they may need more protein to help maintain muscle mass. Some senior dogs may also benefit from a diet that's lower in fat and higher in fiber.

When choosing a dog food, look for one that's labeled as complete and balanced. This means it contains all the nutrients your dog needs in the right proportions. Avoid foods with fillers, artificial colors, and preservatives.

Remember again that every dog is unique, and what works for one dog may not work for another. It's always a good idea to consult with your vet before making any major changes to your dog's diet.

Choosing the right food for your dog's age is an important part of keeping them healthy. By understanding the nutritional needs of puppies, adult dogs, and senior dogs, you can ensure your dog gets the right nutrients at the right time. Remember, a good diet is one of the best gifts you can give your dog for a long, healthy life.

Feeding Schedules and Portion Control

Maintaining a consistent feeding schedule and practicing portion control are two key factors in managing your dog's weight and overall health. These elements of your dog's diet can contribute to their energy levels, digestion, and even their behavior.

A regular feeding schedule is important for dogs. It helps regulate their digestive system and can also play a significant role in house training, particularly for puppies. Most dogs thrive on one or two meals a day, but puppies and some smaller breeds may benefit from more frequent meals.

The timing of meals can depend on your schedule and your dog's needs. Some dogs may prefer to eat in the morning, while others may prefer to eat in the evening. What's most important is to choose a schedule that works for you and stick to it as closely as possible. Consistency can help your dog know what to expect and can contribute to a sense of security and routine.

Portion control is equally important. Overfeeding can lead to obesity, which can cause a host of health problems, including joint issues, diabetes, and heart disease. Conversely, underfeeding can lead to nutritional deficiencies.

The amount you should feed your dog depends on several factors, including their age, size, breed, activity level, and the type of food they're eating. Most commercial dog foods provide feeding guidelines based on weight, but these are just a starting point. Your vet can provide personalized advice based on your dog's individual needs.

When measuring your dog's food, use an actual measuring cup, not a random cup or scoop from your kitchen. This can help ensure accuracy. Remember, the goal is to maintain a healthy weight, not to achieve a certain number on the scale.

It's also important to consider treats and extras in your dog's overall calorie intake. Treats, table scraps, and even some types of medication can add significant calories. As a general rule, treats and extras should make up no more than 10% of your dog's daily calories.

Monitoring your dog's body condition can help you determine whether you're feeding the right amount. You should be able to feel but not see your dog's ribs, and they should have a visible waist when viewed from above.

A consistent feeding schedule and portion control are key components of your dog's diet. By feeding regular meals and the right amount, you can help manage your dog's weight, support their overall health, and even contribute to a happier, more predictable daily routine. Remember, your vet is your best resource for personalized advice about your dog's diet. With their guidance and your commitment, you can ensure your dog gets the nutrition they need to thrive.

Special Diets and Food Sensitivities

Just like humans, dogs can have special dietary needs or food sensitivities. These can arise from a variety of factors, including breed predispositions, underlying health conditions, or individual differences. Understanding these needs can help you provide the best possible nutrition for your dog.

Food sensitivities in dogs can manifest in a variety of ways. Some dogs may experience gastrointestinal symptoms, such as vomiting, diarrhea, or changes in appetite. Others may show signs of skin irritation, such as itching, redness, or hot spots. If you notice any of these symptoms in your dog, it's important to consult with your vet. They can help determine whether a food sensitivity is the cause and guide you in making necessary dietary changes.

Some dogs may benefit from a hypoallergenic diet. These diets are designed to minimize the risk of an allergic reaction and can be particularly helpful for dogs with food allergies or intolerances. Hypoallergenic diets typically use novel proteins and carbohydrates that your dog has not been exposed to before, reducing the chance of an adverse reaction.

Other dogs may require a diet that addresses a specific health condition. For example, dogs with kidney disease may benefit from a diet lower in protein and phosphorus. Dogs with diabetes may require a diet high in fiber and complex carbohydrates. Dogs with pancreatitis may need a low-fat diet. These diets should always be implemented under the guidance of a vet, as they are part of a comprehensive treatment plan for the condition.

Some dogs may simply have a sensitive stomach and do better on a diet that's easy to digest. These diets often feature simple, high-quality ingredients and avoid common irritants, such as artificial colors or flavors.

When transitioning your dog to a new diet, it's important to do so gradually to avoid upsetting their stomach. Start by mixing a small amount of the new food with their current food, and gradually increase the proportion of the new food over a week or two.

It's also important to remember that every dog is unique. What works for one dog may not work for another, even if they have the same condition or sensitivity. Finding the right diet for your dog may involve some trial and error, and what works at one stage of their life may not work at another.

Special diets and food sensitivities are an important aspect of dog nutrition. Whether your dog has a food allergy, a health condition, or simply a sensitive stomach, the right diet can make a big difference in their quality of life. Always consult with your vet before making any major changes to your dog's diet. With their guidance and your commitment, you can find the diet that best meets your dog's unique needs.

Tips for Feeding Senior Dogs

As dogs age, their dietary needs change. Senior dogs often require fewer calories due to decreased activity levels, but they may need more of certain nutrients to support their overall health. Here are some tips for feeding your senior dog to ensure they get the nutrition they need.

Firstly, it's important to monitor your senior dog's weight. Obesity can exacerbate many of the health issues common in older dogs, such as arthritis and heart disease. On the other hand, weight loss can be a sign of an underlying health problem. Regular weigh-ins can help you catch any changes early.

The type of food you feed your senior dog may also need to change. Many dog food companies offer formulas specifically designed for senior dogs. These foods often have fewer calories, more fiber, and an adjusted nutrient profile to support aging bodies. For example, they may have increased levels of omega-3 fatty acids for joint health or added antioxidants for immune support.

However, not all senior dogs are the same. Some may remain active and energetic well into their golden years and may not need a reduced-calorie diet. Others may have health conditions that require specific dietary adjustments. Always consult with your vet before making any major changes to your dog's diet.

Portion control is also crucial for senior dogs. Even if your dog's activity level hasn't changed much, their metabolism may have slowed, and they may not need as much food as they used to. Be sure to adjust their portions accordingly to prevent weight gain.

Dental health becomes increasingly important as dogs age. If your senior dog has dental issues, they may struggle to eat dry kibble. In such cases, wet food can be a good alternative. Dental chews and regular brushing can also help keep your senior dog's teeth healthy.

Hydration is another key aspect of senior dog nutrition. Older dogs may be more prone to dehydration, and some may not drink as much as they should. Wet food can help increase your dog's water intake. Always ensure fresh water is readily available.

Lastly, regular vet check-ups are essential for senior dogs. Your vet can monitor your dog's weight and overall health, perform blood tests to check organ function, and provide personalized dietary advice. They can also help you navigate any health issues that arise and adjust your dog's diet as needed.

Feeding a senior dog involves some special considerations. By monitoring your dog's weight, choosing an appropriate diet, controlling portions, caring for their dental health, ensuring they stay hydrated, and maintaining regular vet check-ups, you can help your senior dog stay healthy and happy in their golden years. Remember, the goal is not just to prolong your dog's life, but to ensure they enjoy a good quality of life in their senior years.

Treats, Snacks, and Healthy Rewards

Treats, snacks, and rewards play a significant role in your dog's diet and training regime. They can be a powerful tool for positive reinforcement, helping you to shape your dog's behavior and strengthen your bond with them. However, it's important to choose these extras wisely and use them in moderation to maintain your dog's health and weight.

When it comes to choosing treats for your dog, quality matters. Look for treats made with wholesome, natural ingredients. Avoid treats with artificial colors, flavors, or preservatives, as these can cause digestive upset or contribute to health issues over time. Also, be mindful of the calorie content. Treats can add up quickly and lead to weight gain if not managed properly.

Healthy alternatives to store-bought treats can often be found right in your kitchen. Many dogs enjoy fruits and vegetables such as carrots, apples, or green beans. These can make low-calorie, nutrient-rich treats. However, always research before feeding your dog any human food to ensure it's safe for them. Some foods, like grapes and onions, are toxic to dogs.

When using treats for training, consider using small, low-calorie treats. This allows you to reward your dog multiple times during a training session without adding too many extra calories to their diet. Some companies offer training treats that are specifically designed to be small and low in calories.

Remember, treats should make up no more than 10% of your dog's daily calorie intake. The rest should come from a balanced, complete diet to ensure your dog gets all the nutrients they need.

Chewing is a natural behavior for dogs and can provide mental stimulation and help with dental health. However, not all chews are created equal. Some can be too hard and risk fracturing your dog's teeth, while others can be a choking hazard or get lodged in the digestive tract. Always supervise your dog when they're enjoying a chew and choose products that are appropriate for your dog's size and chewing style.

Treats, snacks, and rewards can be a beneficial part of your dog's diet and training routine. By choosing high-quality treats, using them in moderation, and considering healthy alternatives, you can use these extras to enrich your dog's diet and strengthen your bond with them. Remember, the best treat you can give your dog is your time and attention. A well-balanced diet, combined with plenty of exercise and love, can help your dog live a long, happy, and healthy life.

CONCLUSION

As we reach the conclusion of this journey, it's important to remember that dog training and care is not a destination, but a continuous journey. The bond you share with your canine companion is something that deepens and evolves over time, enriched by shared experiences, mutual understanding, and the joy of companionship.

Reinforcing training over the years is an essential part of this journey. Training is not a one-time event, but a lifelong commitment. Dogs, like humans, can forget or become rusty on skills if they're not practiced regularly. Consistent reinforcement helps ensure that the behaviors you've worked so hard to establish remain strong.

Remember, positive reinforcement is the key. Celebrate your dog's successes, no matter how small. This not only reinforces the behavior you want to see but also strengthens your bond with your dog. And when challenges arise, as they inevitably will, approach them with patience and understanding. Your dog is not being stubborn or difficult. They're simply trying to understand what you want from them. Your patience and consistency will guide them in the right direction.

Continuing your dog's enrichment and learning is equally important. Dogs are intelligent, curious creatures. They thrive when their minds are stimulated and they have opportunities to learn and explore. This can come in many forms, from puzzle toys and interactive games to new training challenges and experiences.

Remember, enrichment is not just about keeping your dog busy. It's about engaging their mind, stimulating their senses, and providing them with a rich, fulfilling life. Whether it's a new trick, a fun game, or a stimulating toy, these activities can add a whole new dimension to your dog's life.

And finally, the most important part of this journey is to enjoy it. The time you have with your canine companion is precious. Every moment, from the quiet mornings to the playful afternoons and peaceful evenings, is an opportunity to deepen your bond and create lasting memories.

Celebrate your dog's unique personality. Delight in their quirks and individuality. Laugh at their antics. Comfort them in their moments of fear or uncertainty. Cherish the simple moments of companionship, whether it's a peaceful walk in the park or a quiet cuddle on the couch. These are the moments that make the journey worthwhile.

In writing this book, my hope has been to provide you with the knowledge and tools you need to navigate this journey with confidence and joy. I hope the information and advice shared here

Susan White

will serve as a guide, helping you to understand your dog better, train them effectively, and care for them in the best possible way.

But remember, every dog is unique, and there is no one-size-fits-all approach to dog training and care. Listen to your dog. Pay attention to their needs, their preferences, their fears, and their joys. They are your best teacher in this journey.

The journey of dog ownership is one of the most rewarding experiences life has to offer. It's a journey filled with love, learning, challenges, and immeasurable rewards. As you continue on this path, remember to reinforce training, provide ongoing enrichment, and most importantly, enjoy every moment with your canine companion. The bond you share is truly special, and it's something to be cherished every day.

Thank you for allowing me to be a part of your journey. Here's to many happy, healthy, and fulfilling years with your canine companion.

Made in United States
Orlando, FL
14 April 2025